PENGUIN BOOKS — GREAT FOOD

## The Elegant Economist

ELIZA ACTON (1799–1860) was born in Sussex and, apart from some time spent in France, lived for much of her life at Bordyke House in Tonbridge, where she kept house for her mother. *Modern Cookery*, first published in 1845, was her first cookery book and quickly gained wide acclaim for its practical, step-by-step approach. Delia Smith has called Acton 'the best writer of recipes in the English language'.

# The Elegant Economist

ELIZA ACTON

PENGUIN BOOKS

PENGUIN BOOKS

Published by the Penguin Group
Penguin Books Ltd, 80 Strand, London WC2R 0RL, England
Penguin Group (USA) Inc., 375 Hudson Street, New York, New York 10014, USA
Penguin Group (Canada), 90 Eglinton Avenue East, Suite 700, Toronto, Ontario,
Canada M4P 2Y3 (a division of Pearson Penguin Canada Inc.)
Penguin Ireland, 25 St Stephen's Green, Dublin 2, Ireland
(a division of Penguin Books Ltd)
Penguin Group (Australia), 250 Camberwell Road,
Camberwell, Victoria 3124, Australia
(a division of Pearson Australia Group Pty Ltd)
Penguin Books India Pvt Ltd, 11 Community Centre,
Panchsheel Park, New Delhi – 110 017, India
Penguin Group (NZ), 67 Apollo Drive, Rosedale, Auckland 0632, New Zealand
(a division of Pearson New Zealand Ltd)
Penguin Books (South Africa) (Pty) Ltd, 24 Sturdee Avenue,
Rosebank, Johannesburg 2196, South Africa

Penguin Books Ltd, Registered Offices: 80 Strand, London WC2R 0RL, England

www.penguin.com

*Modern Cookery* first published 1845
This extract published in Penguin Books 2011
This edition published for The Book People Ltd, 2011
Hall Wood Avenue, Haydock, St Helens, WA11 9UL

1

All rights reserved

Set in 10.75/13pt Berkeley Oldstyle Book
Typeset by Jouve (UK), Milton Keynes
Printed in Great Britain by Clays Ltd, St Ives plc

Cover design based on a pattern from a plate by Josiah Wedgwood & Sons.
*c.* 1840–50. Lead-glazed earthenware, transfer-printed, painted and gilded
(Photograph copyright © Victoria & Albert Museum.) Picture research by
Samantha Johnson. Lettering by Stephen Raw

ISBN 978–0–141–38971–4

www.greenpenguin.co.uk

# Contents

# Poetic Receipts for Soups, Salads and Dressings

## INGREDIENTS WHICH MAY ALL BE USED FOR MAKING SOUP OF VARIOUS KINDS

Beef – Mutton – Veal – Hams – Salted Pork – Fat Bacon – Pigs' Ears and Feet – Venison – Black and Moor Game – Partridges – Pheasants – Wild Pigeons – Hares – Rabbits – Turkeys – Fowls – Tame Pigeons – Sturgeon – Conger Eel, with all sorts of Fish usually eaten – All Shell-Fish – Every kind of Vegetable and Herb fit for food – Butter – Milk – Eggs – Sago – Arrowroot – Indian Corn – Hominy – Soujee – Tapioca – Pearl Barley – Oatmeal – Polenta – Macaroni – Vermicelli – Semoulina, and other Italian Pastes.

The art of preparing good, wholesome, palatable soups, *without great expense*, which is so well understood in France, and in other countries where they form part of the daily food of all classes of the people, has hitherto been very much neglected in England; yet it really presents no difficulties which a little practice, and the most common degree of care, will not readily overcome; and we strongly recommend increased attention to it, not only on account of the loss and inconvenience which ignorance of it occasions in many households, but because a better knowledge of it will lead naturally to improvement in other branches of cookery connected with it in which our want of skill is now equally apparent.

We have endeavoured to show by the list at the beginning of this chapter the immense number of different articles of which soup may be in turn compounded. It is almost superfluous to add, that it may be rendered at pleasure exceedingly rich, or simple in the extreme; composed, in fact, of all that is most choice in diet, or of little beyond herbs and vegetables.

From the varied produce of a well-stored kitchen garden, it may be made excellent at a very trifling cost; and where fish is fresh and abundant it may be cheaply supplied nearly equal in quality to that for which a full proportion of meat is commonly used.

It is best suited to the colder seasons of the year when thickened well with rice, semoulina, pearl barley, or other ingredients of the same nature; and adapted to the summer months when lighter and more refreshing. Families who have resided much abroad, and those accustomed to continental modes of service, prefer it usually *in any form* to the more solid and heavy dishes which still often supersede it altogether at our tables (except at those of the more affluent classes of society, where it appears, as a matter of course, in the daily bills of fare), and which are so *oppressive*, not only to foreigners, but to all persons generally to whom circumstances have rendered them unaccustomed diet; and many a housekeeper who is compelled by a narrow income to adopt a system of rigid domestic economy, would find it assists greatly in furnishing comfortable meals in a very frugal manner, if the proper modes of making it were fully comprehended as they ought to be.

## TO FRY BREAD TO SERVE WITH SOUP

Cut some slices a quarter of an inch thick from a stale loaf; pare off the crust and divide the bread into dice, or cut it with a small paste-cutter into any other form. For half a pound of bread put two ounces of the best butter into a frying-pan, and when it is quite melted, add the bread; keep it turned over a gentle fire until it is equally coloured to a very pale brown, then drain it from the butter, and dry it on a soft cloth, or on a sheet of paper placed before a clear fire upon a dish, or upon a sieve reversed.

## SIPPETS À LA REINE

Having cut the bread as for common sippets [*see preceding receipt*], spread it on a dish, and pour over it a few spoonsful of thin cream, or of good milk: let it soak for an hour, then fry it in fresh butter of a delicate brown, drain and serve the sippets very hot.

## EXTRACT OF BEEF, OR, VERY STRONG PLAIN BEEF GRAVY SOUP
### (*Baron Liebig's Receipt*)

Take a pound of good, juicy beef (rumpsteak is best for the purpose), from which all the skin and fat that can possibly be separated from it, has been cut away. Chop it up small like sausage-meat; then mix it thoroughly with an exact pint of cold water, and place it on the side of the stove to heat *very slowly indeed*; and give it an occasional stir. It may stand two or three hours before it is allowed to simmer, and will then require at the utmost but fifteen minutes gentle boiling. Professor Liebig directs even less time than this, but the soup then occasionally retains a raw flavour which is distasteful. Salt should be added when the boiling first commences, and for invalids, this, in general, is the only seasoning required. When the extract is thus far prepared, it may be poured from the meat into a basin, and allowed to stand until any particles of fat it may exhibit on the surface can be skimmed off entirely, and the sediment has subsided and left the soup quite clear (which it speedily becomes), when it may be poured gently off, heated in a clean saucepan, and served at once. It will contain all the nutriment which the meat will yield. The scum should always be well cleared from the surface of the soup as it accumulates.

To make light beef tea or broth, merely increase the proportion of water to a pint and a half or a quart; but in all else proceed as above.

Meat (without fat or skin), 1 lb; cold water, exact pint: heating 2 hours or more; to boil 15 minutes at the utmost. Beef tea or broth – Beef, 1 lb; water, 1½ pint or 1 quart.

## CLEAR, PALE GRAVY SOUP, OR CONSOMMÉ

Rub a deep stewpan or soup-pot with butter, and lay into it three quarters of a pound of ham freed entirely from fat, skin, and rust [*crusted salt*], four pounds of leg or neck of veal, and the same weight of lean beef, all cut into thick slices; set it over a clear and rather brisk fire, until the meat is of a fine amber-colour; it must be often moved, and closely watched, that it may not stick to the pan, nor burn. When it is equally browned, lay the bones upon it, and pour in gradually four quarts of boiling water. Take off the scum carefully as it rises, and throw in a pint of cold water at intervals to bring it quickly to the surface. When no more appears, add two ounces of salt, two onions, two large carrots, two turnips, one head of celery, a faggot of savoury herbs, a dozen cloves, half a teaspoonful of whole white pepper, and two large blades of mace. Let the soup boil gently from five hours and a half to six hours and a half: then strain it through a very clean fine cloth, laid in a hair sieve. When it is perfectly cold, remove every particle of fat from the top; and, in taking out the soup, leave the sediment untouched; heat in a clean pan the quantity required for table, add salt to it if needed, and a few drops of chili or of cayenne vinegar. Harvey's sauce, or very fine mushroom catsup, may be substituted for these. When thus prepared the soup is ready to serve: it should be accompanied by pale sippets of fried bread, or sippets *à la reine*. (At tables where English modes of service entirely prevailed, clear gravy-soup, until very recently, was always accompanied by dice, or sippets as they are called, of delicately toasted bread. These are now seldom seen, but some Italian paste, or nicely prepared vegetable, is served *in* the soup instead.) Rice, maccaroni in lengths or in rings, vermicelli, or *nouilles*, may in turn be used to vary it; but they must always be boiled apart, till tender, in broth or water, and well drained before they are slipped into it. The addition of young vegetables, too, and especially of asparagus, will convert it into superior spring-soup; but they, likewise, must be separately cooked.

## VERMICELLI SOUP
### (*Potage au Vermicelle*)

Drop very lightly, and by degrees, six ounces of vermicelli, broken rather small, into three quarts of boiling bouillon, or clear gravy soup; let it simmer for half an hour over a gentle fire, and stir it often. This is the common French mode of making vermicelli soup, and we can recommend it as a particularly good one for family use. In England it is customary to soak, or to blanch the vermicelli, then to drain it well, and to stew it for a shorter time in the soup; the quantity also must be reduced quite two ounces, to suit modern taste.

Bouillon, or gravy soup, 3 quarts; vermicelli, 6 oz; 30 minutes. Or, soup, 3 quarts; vermicelli, 4 oz.; blanched in boiling water 5 minutes; stewed in soup 10 to 15 minutes.

## MADEMOISELLE JENNY LIND'S SOUP
### (*Authentic Receipt*)

This receipt does not merely bear the name of 'Mademoiselle Lind', but is in reality that of the soup which was constantly served to her, as it was prepared by her own cook. We are indebted for it to the kindness of the very popular Swedish authoress, Miss Bremer, who received it direct from her accomplished countrywoman.

The following proportions are for a tureen of this excellent *potage*: Wash a quarter of a pound of the best pearl sago until the water poured from it is clear; then stew it quite tender and very thick in water or thick broth (it will require nearly or quite a quart of liquid, which should be poured to it cold, and heated slowly): then mix gradually with it a pint of good boiling cream, and the yolks of four fresh eggs, and mingle the whole carefully with two quarts of strong veal or beef stock, which should always be kept ready boiling. Send the soup immediately to table.

## THE LORD MAYOR'S SOUP
### (*Author's Receipt*)

We prefer to have this soup made, in part, the evening before it is wanted. Add five quarts of water to the ears and feet [*see ingredients below*]; skim it thoroughly when it first boils, and throw in a tablespoonful of salt, two onions of moderate size, a small head of celery, a bunch of herbs, two whole carrots, a small teaspoonful of white peppercorns, and a blade of mace. Stew these softly until the ears and feet are perfectly tender, and, after they are lifted out, let the liquor be kept *just simmering* only, while they are being boned, that it may not be too much reduced. Put the bones back into it, and stew them as gently as possible for an hour, then strain the soup into a clean pan, and set it by until the morrow in a cool place. The flesh should be cut into dice while it is still warm and covered with the cloth before it becomes *quite* cold. To prepare the soup for table clear the stock from fat and sediment, put it into a very clean stewpan, or deep sauce-pan, and stir to it when it boils, six ounces of the finest rice-flour smoothly mixed with a quarter of a teaspoonful of cayenne, three times as much of mace and salt, the strained juice of a lemon, three tablespoonsful of Harvey's sauce, and half a pint of good sherry or Madeira. Simmer the whole for six or eight minutes, add more salt if needed, stir the soup often, and skim it thoroughly; put in the meat and herbs, and after they have boiled gently for five minutes, dish the soup, add forcemeat-balls or not, at pleasure, and send it to table quickly.

Moderate-sized pigs' feet, 8; ears, 4; water, 5 quarts; salt, 1 tablespoonful; onions, 2; celery, 1 head; carrots, 2; bunch of herbs; peppercorns, 1 small teaspoonful; mace, 1 blade: 3½ to 4½ hours. Stock, 5 pints; rice-flour, 6 oz; cayenne, ¼ teaspoonful; mace and salt, each ¾ of a teaspoonful; juice of 1 lemon; Harvey's sauce, 3 tablespoonsful; sherry or Madeira, ½ pint: 6 to 8 minutes. Savoury herbs, 2 tablespoonsful: 5 minutes.

*Obs. 1.* Should the quantity of stock exceed five pints, an additional ounce or more of rice must be used, and the flavouring be altogether increased in proportion. Of the minced herbs, two-thirds should be parsley, and the remainder equal parts of lemon thyme and winter savoury, unless sweet basil should be at hand, when a teaspoonful of it may be substituted for half of the parsley. To some tastes a seasoning of sage would be acceptable; and a slice or two of lean ham will much improve the flavour of the soup.

## APPLE SOUP
### (*Soupe à la Bourguignon*)

Clear the fat from five pints of good mutton broth, *bouillon*, or shin of beef stock, and strain it through a fine sieve; add to it when it boils, a pound and a half of good cooking apples, and stew them down in it very softly to a smooth pulp; press the whole through a strainer, add a small teaspoonful of powdered ginger and plenty of pepper, simmer the soup for a couple of minutes, skim, and serve it very hot, accompanied by a dish of rice, boiled as for curries.

Broth, 5 pints; apples, 1½ lb: 25 to 40 minutes. Ginger, 1 teaspoonful; pepper, ½ teaspoonful: 2 minutes.


## PARSNEP SOUP

Dissolve, over a gentle fire, four ounces of good butter, in a wide stewpan or saucepan, and slice in directly two pounds of sweet tender parsneps; let them stew very gently until all are quite soft, then pour in gradually sufficient veal stock or good broth to cover them, and boil the whole slowly from twenty minutes to half an hour; work it with a wooden spoon through a fine sieve, add as much stock as will make two quarts in all, season the soup with salt and white pepper or cayenne, give it one boil, skim, and serve it very hot. Send pale fried sippets to table with it.

Butter, 4 oz; parsnep, 2 lb: ¾ hour, or more. Stock, 1 quart: 20 to 30 minutes; 1 full quart more of stock; pepper, salt: 1 minute.

*Obs.* We can particularly recommend this soup to those who like the peculiar flavour of the vegetable.

## TO BOIL RICE FOR MULLAGATAWNY SOUPS, OR FOR CURRIES

The Patna, or small-grained rice, which is not so good as the Carolina, for the general purposes of cookery, ought to be served with currie. First take out the unhusked grains, then wash the rice in several waters, and put it into a large quantity of cold water: bring it gently to boil, keeping it uncovered, and boil it softly for fifteen minutes, when it will be perfectly tender, and every grain will remain distinct. Throw it into a *large* cullender, and let it drain for ten minutes near the fire; should it not then appear *quite* dry, turn it into a dish, and set it for a short time into a gentle oven, or let it steam in a clean saucepan near the fire. It should neither be stirred, except just at first, to prevent its lumping while it is still quite hard, nor touched with either fork or spoon; the stewpan may be shaken occasionally, should the rice seem to require it, and it should be thrown lightly from the cullender upon the dish. A couple of minutes before it is done, throw in some salt, and from the time of its beginning to boil remove the scum as it rises.

Patna rice, ½ lb; cold water, 2 quarts: boiled slowly, 15 minutes. Salt, 1 large teaspoonful.

*Obs.* This, of all the modes of boiling rice which we have tried, and they have been very numerous, is indisputably the best. The Carolina rice answers well dressed in the same manner, but requires four or five minutes longer boiling: it should never be served until it is quite tender. One or two minutes, more or less, will sometimes, from the varying quality of the grain, be requisite to render it tender.

## GOOD VEGETABLE MULLAGATAWNY

Dissolve in a large stewpan or thick iron saucepan, four ounces of butter, and when it is on the point of browning, throw in four large mild onions sliced, three pounds' weight of young vegetable marrow cut in large dice and cleared from the skin and seeds, four large or six moderate-sized cucumbers, pared, split, and emptied likewise of their seeds, and from three to six large acid apples, according to the taste; shake the pan often, and stew these over a gentle fire until they are tolerably tender; then strew lightly over and mix well amongst them, three heaped tablespoonsful of mild currie powder, with nearly a third as much of salt, and let the vegetables stew from twenty to thirty minutes longer; then pour to them gradually sufficient boiling water (broth or stock if preferred) to just cover them, and when they are reduced almost to a pulp press the whole through a hair-sieve with a wooden spoon, and heat it in a clean stewpan, with as much additional liquid as will make two quarts with that which was first added. Give any flavouring that may be needed, whether of salt, cayenne, or acid, and serve the soup extremely hot. Should any butter appear on the surface, let it be carefully skimmed off, or stir in a small dessertspoonful of arrowroot (smoothly mixed with a little cold broth or water) to absorb it. Rice may be served with this soup at pleasure, but as it is of the consistence of winter peas soup, it scarcely requires any addition. The currie powder may be altogether omitted for variety, and the whole converted into a plain vegetable *potage*; or it may be rendered one of high savour, by browning all the vegetables lightly, and adding to them rich brown stock. Tomatas, when in season, may be substituted for the apples, after being divided, and freed from their seeds.

Butter, 4 oz; vegetable marrow, pared and scooped, 3 lb; large mild onions, 4; large cucumbers, 4; or middling-sized, 6; apples, or large tomatas, 3 to 6: 30 to 40 minutes. Mild currie-powder, 3 heaped tablespoonsful; salt, one small tablespoonful: 20 to 32 minutes. Water, broth, or good stock, 2 quarts.

## CHEAP FISH SOUPS

An infinite variety of excellent soups may be made of fish, which may be stewed down for them in precisely the same manner as meat, and with the same addition of vegetables and herbs. When the skin is coarse or rank it should be carefully stripped off before the fish is used; and any oily particles which may float on the surface should be entirely removed from it.

In France, Jersey, Cornwall, and many other localities, the conger eel, divested of its skin, is sliced up into thick cutlets and made into soup, which we are assured by English families who have it often served at their tables, is extremely good. A half-grown fish is best for the purpose. After the soup has been strained and allowed to settle, it must be heated afresh, and rice and minced parsley may be added to it, or it may be thickened with rice-flour only, or served clear. Curried fish-soups, too, are much to be recommended.

When broth or stock has been made as above with conger eel, common eels, whitings, haddocks, codlings, fresh water fish, or any common kind, which may be at hand, flakes of cold salmon, cod fish, John Dories, or scallops of cold soles, plaice, etc.,* may be heated and served in it; and the remains of crabs or lobsters mingled with them. The large oysters sold at so cheap a rate upon the coast, and which are not much esteemed for eating raw, serve admirably for imparting flavour to soup, and the softer portions of them may be served in it after a few minutes of gentle simmering. Anchovy or any other store fish-sauce may be added with good effect to many of these pottages if used with moderation. Prawns and shrimps likewise would generally be considered an improvement to them.

For more savoury preparations, fry the fish and vegetables, lay them into the soup-pot, and add boiling, instead of cold water to them.

## COLD DUTCH OR AMERICAN SAUCE, FOR SALADS OF DRESSED VEGETABLES, SALT FISH, OR HARD EGGS

Put into a saucepan three ounces of good butter very smoothly blended with a quite small teaspoonful of

---

* Cold vegetables, cut up small, may be added with these at pleasure.

flour, and add to them a large wineglassful of cold water, half as much sharp vinegar (or very fresh, strained, lemon-juice) a saltspoonful of salt, and half as much cayenne in fine powder. Keep these shaken briskly round, or stirred over a clear fire, until they form a smooth sauce and boil rapidly; then stir them very quickly to the beaten yolks of four fresh eggs, which will immediately give the sauce the consistence of custard; pour it hot over the salad, and place it on ice, or in a very cool larder until it is quite cold: if properly made, it will be very thick and smooth, and slightly *set*, as if it contained a small portion of isinglass. A dessertspoonful of parsley – or of tarragon – can be mingled with it at *pleasure*, or any flavour given to it with store-sauces which is liked. It converts flakes of salt-fish, sliced potatoes (new or old), and hard eggs, into excellent salads.

## ENGLISH SAUCE FOR SALAD, COLD MEAT, OR COLD FISH

The first essential for a smooth, well-made English salad dressing is to have the yolks of the eggs used for it sufficiently hard to be reduced easily to a perfect paste. They should be boiled at least fifteen minutes, and should have become *quite* cold before they are taken from the shells; they should also be well covered with water when they are cooked, or some parts of them will be tough, and will spoil the appearance of the sauce by rendering it lumpy, unless they be worked through a sieve, a process which is always better avoided if possible. To a couple of yolks broken up and mashed to a paste with the back of a wooden spoon, add a small saltspoonful of salt, a large one of pounded sugar, a few grains of fine cayenne, and a teaspoonful of cold water; mix these well, and stir to them by degrees a quarter of a pint of sweet cream; throw in next, stirring the sauce briskly, a tablespoonful of strong chili vinegar, and add as much common or French vinegar as will acidulate the mixture agreeably. A tablespoonful of either will be sufficient for many tastes, but it is easy to increase the proportion when more is liked. Six tablespoonsful of olive oil, of the purest quality, may be substituted for the cream: it should be added in very small portions to the other ingredients and stirred briskly as each is added until the sauce resembles custard. When this is used, the water should be omitted. The piquancy of this preparation – which is very delicate, made by the directions just given – may be heightened by the addition of a little eschalot vinegar, Harvey's sauce, essence of anchovies, French mustard, or tarragon vinegar: or by bruising with the eggs a morsel of garlic, half the size of a hazel-nut: it should always, however, be rendered as appropriate as may be to the dish with which it is to be served.

*Obs.* As we have before had occasion to remark, garlic, when very sparingly and judiciously used, imparts a remarkably fine savour to a sauce or gravy, and neither a strong nor a coarse one, as it does when used in larger quantities. The veriest morsel (or, as the French call it, a mere *soupçon*) of the root, is sufficient to give this agreeable piquancy, but unless the proportion be extremely small, the effect will be quite different. The Italians dress their salads upon a round of delicately toasted bread, which is rubbed with garlic, saturated with oil, and sprinkled with cayenne, before it is laid into the bowl: they also eat the bread thus prepared, but with less of oil, and untoasted often, before their meals as a digester.

## THE POET'S RECEIPT FOR SALAD

*Two large potatoes, passed through kitchen sieve*
*Unwonted softness to the salad give;*
*Of mordent mustard, add a single spoon,*
*Distrust the condiment which bites so soon;*
*But deem it not, thou man of herbs, a fault,*
*To add a double quantity of salt;*
*Three times the spoon with oil of Lucca crown,*
*And once with vinegar, procured from town;*
*True flavour needs it, and your poet begs*
*The pounded yellow of two well-boiled eggs;*
*Let onion atoms lurk within the bowl,*
*And, scarce suspected, animate the whole;*
*And lastly, in the flavoured compound toss*
*A magic teaspoon of anchovy sauce:*
*Then, though green turtle fail, though venison's tough,*
*And ham and turkey are not boiled enough,*
*Serenely full, the epicure may say –*
*Fate cannot harm me – I have dined today.*

Two well-boiled potatoes, passed through a sieve; a teaspoonful of mustard; two teaspoonsful of salt; one of essence of anchovy; about a quarter of a teaspoonful of very finely-chopped onions, well bruised into the mixture; three tablespoonsful of oil; one of vinegar; the yolks of two eggs, hard boiled. Stir up the salad immediately before dinner, and stir it up thoroughly.

N.B. As this salad is the result of great experience and reflection, it is hoped young salad makers will not attempt to make any improvements upon it.


## OXFORD BRAWN SAUCE

Mingle thoroughly a tablespoonful of brown sugar with a teaspoonful of made mustard, a third as much of salt, some pepper, from three to four tablespoonsful of very fine salad-oil, and two of strong vinegar: or apportion the same ingredients otherwise to the taste.


## ENGLISH SALADS

The herbs and vegetables for a salad cannot be too freshly gathered: they should be carefully cleared from insects and washed with scrupulous nicety; they are better when not prepared until near the time of sending them to table, and should not be sauced until the instant before they are served. Tender lettuces, of which the stems should be cut off, and the outer leaves be stripped away, mustard and cress, young radishes, and occasionally chives or small green onions (when the taste of a party is in favour of these last) are the usual ingredients of summer salads. (In early spring, as we have stated in another chapter, the young white leaves of the dandelion will supply a very wholesome and excellent salad, of which the slight bitterness is to many persons as agreeable as that of the endive.) Half-grown cucumbers sliced thin, and mixed with them, are a favourite addition with many persons. In England it is customary to cut the lettuces extremely fine: the French, who object to the *flavour of the knife*, which they fancy this mode imparts, break them small instead. Young celery alone, sliced, and dressed with a rich salad mixture, is excellent: it is still in some families served thus always with roast pheasants.

Beetroot, baked or boiled, blanched endive, small salad-herbs which are easily raised at any time of the year, celery, and hardy lettuces, with any ready-dressed vegetable, will supply salads through the winter. Cucumber vinegar is an agreeable addition to these.

## FRENCH SALAD

In winter this is made principally of beautifully-blanched endive, washed delicately clean and broken into small branches with the fingers, then taken from the water and shaken dry in a basket of peculiar form, appropriated to the purpose,* or in a fine cloth; then arranged in the salad bowl, and strewed with herbs (tarragon generally, when in season) minced small: the dressing is not added until just before the salad is eaten. In summer, young lettuces are substituted for the endive, and intermixed with a variety of herbs, some of which are not generally cultivated in England.

* Salad-baskets are also to be found in many good English kitchens, but they are not in such general use here as on the Continent.

## FRENCH SALAD DRESSING

Stir a saltspoonful of salt and half as much pepper into a large spoonful of oil, and when the salt is dissolved, mix with them four additional spoonsful of oil, and pour the whole over the salad; let it be *well* turned, and then add a couple of spoonsful of tarragon vinegar; mix the whole thoroughly, and serve it without delay. The salad should not be dressed in this way until the instant before it is wanted for table: the proportions of salt and pepper can be increased at pleasure, and common or cucumber vinegar may be substituted for the tarragon, which, however, is more frequently used in France than any other.

Salt, 1 spoonful: pepper, ½ as much; oil, 5 salad-spoonsful; tarragon, or other vinegar, 2 spoonsful.

## AN EXCELLENT HERRING SALAD
### (*Swedish Receipt*)

Soak, skin, split, and bone a large Norway herring; lay the two sides along a dish, and slice them slopingly (or substitute for this one or two fine Dutch herring). Arrange in symmetrical order over the fish slices of cooked beetroot, cold boiled potatoes, and pickled gherkins; then add one or two sharp apples chopped small, and the yolks and whites, separately minced, of some hard-boiled eggs, with any thing else which may be at hand, and may serve to vary tastefully the decoration of the dish. Place these ingredients in small heaps of well-contrasting colours on the surface of the salad, and lay a border of curled celery leaves or parsley round the bowl.

For sauce, rub the yolk of one hard-boiled egg quite smooth with some salt; to this add oil and vinegar as for an ordinary salad, and dilute the whole with some thick sour cream.

*Obs.* 'Sour cream' is an ingredient not much approved by English taste, but it enters largely into German cookery, and into that of Sweden, and of other northern countries also. About half a pound of cold beef cut into small thin shavings or collops, is often added to a herring salad abroad: it may be either of simply roasted or boiled, or of salted and smoked meat.

# Beef, Mutton, Lamb and Pork

## FRENCH BEEF À LA MODE
### (*A common Receipt*)

Take seven or eight pounds of a rump of beef (or of any other tender joint), free from bone, and skewer it firmly into a good shape. Put two ounces of butter into a thick saucepan or stewpan, and when it boils stir to it a table-spoonful of flour; keep these well shaken over a gentle fire until they are of a fine amber colour; then lay in the beef, and brown it on both sides, taking care that it shall not stick to the pan. Pour to it by slow degrees, letting each portion boil before the next is added or the butter will float upon the surface and be difficult to clear off afterwards, three-quarters of a pint of hot water or gravy; add a bunch of savoury herbs, one large or two small carrots cut in thick slices, two or three moderate-sized onions, two bay leaves, and sufficient pepper and salt to season the gravy. Let the meat simmer gently from four to five hours, and turn it when it is half done. When ready to serve, lift the beef into a hot dish, lay the vegetables round, and pour the gravy over it, after having taken out the herbs and skimmed away the fat. In France, half or the whole of a calf's foot is stewed with the beef, which is there generally larded with thick lardoons of fat bacon. Veal dressed in this way is even better than beef.

The stewpan used for either should be as nearly of the size of the meat as possible.

Beef, 7 to 8 lb: 4 to 5 hours.

## SPICED BEEF
### (*Good and wholesome*)

For twelve pounds of the round, rump, or thick flank of beef, take a large teaspoonful of freshly-pounded mace, and of ground black pepper, twice as much of cloves, one small nutmeg, and a quarter of a teaspoonful of cayenne, all in the finest powder. Mix them *well* with seven ounces of brown sugar, rub the beef with them and let it lie three days; add to it then half a pound of fine salt, and rub and turn it once in twenty-four hours for twelve days. Just wash, but do not soak it; skewer, or bind it into good form, put it into a stewpan or saucepan nearly of its size, pour to it a pint and a half of good beef broth, and when it begins to boil, take off the scum, and throw in one small onion, a moderate-sized faggot of thyme and parsley, and two large, or four small carrots. Let it simmer quite softly for four hours and a half, and if not wanted to serve hot, leave it in its own liquor until it is nearly cold. This is an excellent and far more wholesome dish than the hard bright-coloured beef which is cured with large quantities of salt and saltpetre; two or three ounces of juniper-berries may be added to it with the spice, to heighten its flavour.

Beef, 12 lb; sugar, 7 oz; mace and black pepper, each, 1 large teaspoonful; cloves, in powder, 1 large dessert-spoonful; nutmeg, 1; cayenne, ¼ teaspoonful: 3 days.

Fine salt, ½ lb: 12 days. Beef broth (or bouillon), 1½ pint; onion, 1 small; bunch of herbs; carrots, 2 large, or 4 small: stewed 4½ hours.

*Obs.* We give this receipt *exactly* as we have often had it used, but celery and turnips might be added to the gravy; and when the appearance of the meat is much considered, three-quarters of an ounce of saltpetre may be mixed with the spices; the beef may also be plainly boiled in water only, with a few vegetables, or baked in a deep pan with a little gravy. No meat must ever be left to cool in the stewpan or saucepan in which it is cooked; it must be lifted into a pan of its own depth, and the liquor poured upon it.

## BEEF ROLL, OR CANELLON DE BŒUF
### (Entrée)

Chop and mix thoroughly two pounds of lean and very tender beef with one pound of slightly striped bacon; season them with a large teaspoonful of pepper, a little salt, a small nutmeg, or two-thirds as much mace, the grated rind of a lemon, or a teaspoonful of thyme and parsley finely minced. Form the whole into a thick rouleau, wrap a buttered paper round it, enclose it in a paste made of flour and water, and send it to a moderate oven for a couple of hours. Remove the paper and the crust and serve the meat with a little brown gravy. Lamb and veal are excellent dressed in this way, particularly when mixed with plenty of mushrooms. Brown cucumber sauce should be served with the lamb; and currie, or oyster sauce, when there are no mushrooms, with the veal. A flavouring of onion or of eschalot, where it is liked, can be added at pleasure to the beef; suet, or the fat of the meat, may be substituted for the bacon.

Beef, 2 lb; bacon, 1 lb; pepper ¼ oz; little salt; small nutmeg; rind of 1 lemon, or savoury herbs, 1 teaspoonful: baked 2 hours.

## BRESLAW OF BEEF
### (*Good*)

Trim the brown edges from half a pound of undressed roast beef, shred it small, and mix it with four ounces of fine bread-crumbs, a teaspoonful of minced parsley, and two-thirds as much of thyme, two ounces of butter broken small, half a cupful of gravy or cream, a high sea-soning of pepper and cayenne and mace or nutmeg, a small teaspoonful of salt, and three large eggs well whisked. Melt a little butter in a deep dish, pour in the beef, and bake it half an hour; turn it out, and send it to table with brown gravy in a tureen. When cream or gravy is not at hand, an additional egg or two and rather more butter must be used. We think that grated lemon-rind improves the breslaw. A portion of fat from the joint can be added where it is liked. The mixture is sometimes baked in buttered cups.

Beef, ½ lb; bread-crumbs, 4 oz; butter, 2 oz; gravy or cream, ½ cupful; parsley, 1 teaspoonful; thyme, two-thirds of teaspoonful; eggs, 3 or 4, if small; salt, 1 teaspoonful; pepper and nutmeg, ½ teaspoonful each: bake ½ hour.

## NORMAN HASH

Peel and fry two dozens of button onions in butter until they are lightly browned, then stir to them a tablespoonful of flour, and when the whole is of a deep amber shade, pour in a wineglassful and a half of red wine, and a large cup of boiling broth or water; add a seasoning of salt and common pepper or cayenne, and a little lemon-pickle catsup or lemon-juice, and boil the whole until the onions are quite tender; cut and trim into small handsome slices the remains of either a roast or boiled joint of beef, and arrange them in a clean saucepan; pour the gravy and onions on them, and let them stand for a while to imbibe the flavour of the sauce; then place the hash near the fire, and when it is thoroughly hot serve it immediately, without allowing it to boil.

## ROAST SADDLE OF MUTTON

This is an excellent joint, though not considered a very economical one. It is usual for the butcher to raise the skin from it before it is sent in, and to skewer it on again, that in the roasting the juices of the meat may be better preserved, and the fat prevented from taking too much colour, as this should be but delicately browned. In less than half an hour before the mutton is done, remove the skin, and flour the joint lightly after having basted it well. Our own great objection to frothed meat would lead us to recommend that the skin should be taken off half an hour earlier, and that the joint should be kept at sufficient distance from the fire to prevent the possibility of the fat being burned; and that something more of time should be allowed for the roasting. With constant basting, great care, and good management, the cook may always ensure the proper appearance of this, or of any other joint (except, perhaps, of a haunch of venison) without having recourse to papering or pasting, or even to replacing the skin; but when unremitted attention cannot be given to this one part of the dinner, it is advisable to take all precautions that can secure it from being spoiled.

2½ to 2¾ hours. More if *very* large.


## ROAST NECK OF MUTTON

This is a very favourite joint in many families [*and contains the cutlets, as opposed to the chops of the loin*], the flesh being more tender and succulent than that even of the loin; and when only a small roast is required, the best end of the neck of mutton, or the middle, if divested of a large portion of the fat and cut into good shape, will furnish one of appropriate size and of excellent quality. Let the ends be cut quite even and the bones short, so as to give a handsome squareness of form to the meat. The butcher, if directed to do so, will chop off the chine bone, and divide the long bones sufficiently at the joints to prevent any difficulty in separating them at table. From four to five pounds weight of the neck will require from an hour to an hour and a quarter of roasting at a clear and brisk, but not *fierce*, fire. It should be placed at a distance until it is heated through, and then moved nearer, and kept *thoroughly basted* until it is done. Tomatas baked or roasted may be sent to table with it; or a little plain gravy and red currant jelly; or it may be served without either.

When the entire joint, with the exception of the scragend (which should always be taken off), is cooked, proportionate time must be allowed for it.

## THE CAVALIER'S BROIL

Half roast or stew, or parboil, a small, or moderate-sized shoulder of mutton; lift it into a hot dish, score it on both sides down to the bone, season it well with fine salt and cayenne or pepper, and finish cooking it upon the gridiron over a brisk fire. Skim the fat from any gravy that may have flowed from it, and keep the dish which contains it quite hot to receive the joint again. Warm a cupful of pickled mushrooms, let a part of them be minced, and strew them over the broil when it is ready to be served; arrange the remainder round it, and send it instantly to table. The reader will scarcely need to be told that this is an excellent dish.

## CHINA CHILO

Mince a pound of an undressed loin or leg of mutton, with or without a portion of its fat; mix with it two or three young lettuces shred small, a pint of young peas, a teaspoonful of salt, half as much pepper, four tablespoonsful of water, from two to three ounces of good butter, and, if the flavour be liked, a few green onions minced. Keep the whole well stirred with a fork over a clear and gentle fire until it is quite hot, then place it closely covered by the side of the stove, or on a high trivet, that it may stew as softly as possible for a couple of hours. One or even two half-grown cucumbers, cut small by scoring the ends deeply as they are sliced, or a quarter-pint of minced mushrooms may be added with good effect; or a dessertspoonful of currie-powder and a large chopped onion. A dish of boiled rice should be sent to table with it.

Mutton, 1 pound; green peas, 1 pint; young lettuces, 2; salt, 1 teaspoonful; pepper, ½ teaspoonful; water, 4 tablespoonsful; butter, 2 to 3 oz: 2 hours. Varieties: cucumbers, 2; or mushrooms minced, ¼ pint; or currie-powder, 1 dessertspoonful, and 1 large onion.

## SADDLE OF LAMB

This is an exceedingly nice joint for a small party. It should be roasted at a brisk fire, and kept constantly basted with its own dripping: it will require from an hour and three-quarters to two hours roasting. Send it to table with mint sauce, brown cucumber sauce, and a salad.

1¾ to 2 hours.

*Obs.* The following will be found an excellent receipt for mint sauce: With three heaped tablespoonsful of finely-chopped young mint, mix two of pounded and sifted sugar, and six of the best vinegar; stir it until the sugar is dissolved.

## TO ROAST A SUCKING PIG

After the pig has been scalded and prepared for the spit, wipe it as dry as possible, and put into the body about half a pint of fine bread-crumbs, mixed with three heaped teaspoonsful of sage, minced very small, three ounces of good butter, a large saltspoonful of salt, and two-thirds as much of pepper or some cayenne. Sew it up with soft, but strong cotton; truss it as a hare, with the fore legs skewered back, and the hind ones forward; lay it to a strong clear fire, but keep it at a moderate distance, as it would quickly blister or scorch if placed too near. So soon as it has become warm, rub it with a bit of butter tied in a fold of muslin or of thin cloth, and repeat this process constantly while it is roasting. When the gravy begins to drop from it, put basins or small deep tureens under, to catch it in.* As soon as the pig is of a fine light amber brown and the steam draws strongly towards the fire, wipe it quite dry with a clean cloth, and rub a bit of cold butter over it. When it is half done, a pig iron, or in lieu of this, a large flat iron should be hung in the centre of the grate, or the middle of the pig will be done long before the ends. When it is ready for table lay it into a very hot dish, and before the spit is withdrawn, take off and open the head and split the body in two; chop together quickly the stuffing and the brains, put them into half-pint of good veal gravy ready thickened, add a glass of Madeira or of sherry and the

---

* A deep oblong dish of suitable size seems better adapted to this purpose.

gravy which has dropped from the pig; pour a small portion of this under the roast and serve the remainder as hot as possible in a tureen: a little pounded mace and cayenne with a squeeze of lemon-juice, may be added, should the flavour require heightening. Fine bread sauce, and plain gravy should likewise be served with it. Some persons still prefer the old-fashioned currant sauce to any other: and many have the brains and stuffing stirred into rich melted butter, instead of gravy; but the receipt which we have given has usually been so much approved, that we can recommend it with some confidence, as it stands. Modern taste would perhaps be rather in favour of rich brown gravy and thick tomata sauce.

In dishing the pig lay the body flat in the middle, and the head and ears at the ends and sides. When very pure oil can be obtained, it is preferable to butter for the basting: it should be laid on with a bunch of feathers. A pig of three weeks old is considered as best suited to the table, and it should always be dressed if possible the day it is killed.

1¼ to 1¾ hour.

## TO BOIL A HAM

The degree of soaking which must be given to a ham before it is boiled, must depend both on the manner in which it has been cured, and on its age. If highly salted, hard, and old, a day and night, or even longer, may be requisite to dilate the pores sufficiently, and to extract a portion of the salt. To do either effectually the water must be several times changed during the steeping. After the ham has been scraped, or brushed, as clean as possible, pare away lightly any part which, from being blackened or rusty, would disfigure it; though it is better *not* to cut the flesh at all unless it be really requisite for the good appearance of the joint. Lay it into a ham-kettle, or into any other vessel of a similar form, and cover it plentifully with cold water; bring it *very slowly* to boil, and clear off carefully the scum which will be thrown up in great abundance. So soon as the water has been cleared from this, draw back the pan quite to the edge of the stove, that the ham may be simmered softly but steadily, until it is tender. On no account allow it to boil fast. A bunch of herbs and three or four carrots, thrown in directly after the water has been skimmed, will improve it. When it can be probed very easily with a sharp skewer, or larding-pin, lift it out, strip off the skin, and should there be an oven at hand, set it in for a few minutes after having laid it on a drainer; strew fine raspings over it, or grate a hard-toasted crust, unless it is to be glazed, when neither of these must be used.

Small ham, 3½ to 4 hours; moderate sized, 4 to 4½ hours; very large, 5 to 5½ hours.

*Obs.* We have seen the following manner of boiling a ham recommended, but we have not tried it: 'Put into the water in which it is to be boiled, a quart of old cider and a pint of vinegar, a large bunch of sweet herbs, and a bay leaf. When it is two-thirds done, skin, cover it with raspings, and set it in an oven until it is done enough: it will prove incomparably superior to a ham boiled in the usual way.'

## TO BAKE A HAM

Unless when too salt from not being sufficiently soaked, a ham (particularly a young and fresh one) eats much better baked than boiled, and remains longer good. The safer plan to ensure its being sufficiently steeped, is to lay it into plenty of cold water over night. The following day soak it for an hour or more in warm water, wash it delicately clean, trim smoothly off all rusty parts, and lay it with the rind downwards into a large common pie-dish; press an oiled paper closely over it, and then fasten securely to the edge of the dish a *thick* cover of coarse paste; and send the ham to a moderate oven, of which the heat will be well sustained until it is baked. Or, when more convenient, lay the ham at once – rind downwards – on the paste, of which sufficient should be made, and rolled off to an inch in thickness, to completely envelop it. Press a sheet of oiled foolscap paper upon it; gather up the paste firmly all round, draw and pinch the edges together, and fold them over on the upper side of the ham, taking care to close them so that no gravy can escape. Send it to a well-heated, but not a fierce oven. A very small ham will require quite three hours baking, and a large one five. The crust and the skin must be removed while it is hot. When part only of the ham is dressed, this mode is better far than boiling it.

## EXCELLENT SAUSAGES

Chop, first separately, and then together, one pound and a quarter of veal, perfectly free from fat, skin, and sinew, with an equal weight of lean pork, and of the inside fat of the pig. Mix well, and strew over the meat an ounce and a quarter of salt, half an ounce of pepper, one nutmeg grated, and a *large* teaspoonful of pounded mace. Turn, and chop the sausages until they are equally seasoned throughout, and tolerably fine; press them into a clean pan, and keep them in a very cool place. Form them, when wanted for table, into cakes something less than an inch thick; and flour and fry them then for about ten minutes in a little butter, or roast them in a Dutch or American oven.

Lean of veal and pork, of each 1 lb 4 oz; fat of pork, 1 lb 4 oz; salt, 1¼ oz; pepper, ½ oz; nutmeg, 1; mace, 1 *large* teaspoonful: fried in cakes, 10 minutes.

## SAUSAGES AND CHESTNUTS
### (*Entrée – An excellent dish – French*)

Roast, and take the husk and skin from forty fine Spanish chestnuts; fry gently, in a morsel of butter, six small flat oval cakes of fine sausage-meat, and when they are well browned, lift them out and pour into a saucepan, which should be bright in the inside, the greater part of the fat in which they have been fried; mix with it a large teaspoonful of flour, and stir these over the fire till they are well and equally browned; then pour in by degrees nearly a half-pint of strong beef or veal broth, or gravy, and two glasses of good white wine; add a *small* bunch of savoury herbs, and as much salt and pepper, or cayenne, as will season the whole properly; give it a boil, lay in the sausages round the pan, and the chestnuts in the centre; stew them *very* softly for nearly an hour; take out the herbs, dish the sausages neatly and heap the chestnuts in the centre, strain the sauce over them and serve them very hot. There should be no sage mixed with the pork to dress thus.

Chestnuts roasted, 40; sausages, 6; gravy, nearly ½ pint; sherry or Madeira, 2 wineglassesful: stewed together from 50 to 60 minutes.

## TRUFFLED SAUSAGES
### (*Saucisses aux Truffes*)

With two pounds of the lean of young tender pork, mix one pound of fat, a quarter of a pound of truffles, minced very small, an ounce and a half of salt, a seasoning of cayenne, or quite half an ounce of white pepper, a nutmeg, a teaspoonful of freshly pounded mace, and a dessertspoonful or more of savoury herbs dried and reduced to powder. Test a morsel of the mixture; heighten any of the seasonings to the taste; and put the meat into delicately clean skins: if it be for immediate use, and the addition is liked, moisten it, before it is dressed, with one or two glassesful of Madeira. The substitution of a clove of garlic for the truffles, will convert these into *Saucisses à l'Ail*, or garlic sausages.

# Poultry and Game:
## Seasonal or Perennial

### TO BONE A FOWL OR TURKEY
### WITHOUT OPENING IT

After the fowl has been drawn and singed, wipe it inside and out with a clean cloth, but do not wash it. Take off the head, cut through the skin all round the first joint of the legs, and pull them from the fowl, to draw out the large tendons. Raise the flesh first from the lower part of the back-bone, and a little also from the end of the breast-bone, if necessary; work the knife gradually to the socket of the thigh; with the point of the knife detach the joint from it, take the end of the bone firmly in the fingers, and cut the flesh clean from it down to the next joint, round which pass the point of the knife carefully, and when the skin is loosened from it in every part, cut round the next bone, keeping the edge of the knife close to it, until the whole of the leg is done. Remove the bones of the other leg in the same manner; then detach the flesh from the back and breast-bone sufficiently to enable you to reach the upper joints of the wings; proceed with these as with the legs, but be especially careful not to pierce the skin of the second joint. It is usual to leave the pinions unboned, in order to give more easily its natural form to the fowl when it is dressed. The merrythought [*wishbone*] and neck-bones may now easily

35

be cut away, the back- and side-bones taken out without being divided, and the breast bone separated carefully from the flesh (which, as the work progresses, must be turned back from the bones upon the fowl, until it is completely inside out). After the one remaining bone is removed, draw the wings and legs back to their proper form, and turn the fowl right side outwards.

A turkey is boned exactly in the same manner, but as it requires a very large proportion of forcemeat to fill it entirely, the legs and wings are sometimes drawn into the body, to diminish the expense of this. If very securely trussed, and sewn, the bird may be either boiled, or stewed in rich gravy, as well as roasted, after being boned and forced; but it must be most gently cooked, or it may burst.


## TO BROIL A CHICKEN OR FOWL

Either of these, when merely split and broiled, is very dry and unsavoury eating; but will be greatly improved if first boiled gently from five to ten minutes and left to become cold, then divided, dipped into egg and well seasoned bread-crumbs, plentifully sprinkled with clarified butter, dipped again into the crumbs, and broiled over a clear and gentle fire from half to three-quarters of an hour. It should be served very hot, with mushroom-sauce or with a little good plain gravy, which may be thickened and flavoured with a teaspoonful of mushroom-powder mixed with half as much flour and a little butter; or with some *Espagnole*. It should be opened at the back, and evenly divided quite through; the legs should be trussed like those of a boiled fowl; the breast-bone, or that of the back may be removed at pleasure, and both sides of the bird should be made as flat as they can be that the fire may penetrate every part equally: the inside should be first laid towards it. The neck, feet and gizzard may be boiled down with a small quantity of onion and carrot, previously browned in a morsel of butter to make the gravy; and the liver, after having been simmered with them for five or six minutes, may be used to thicken it after it is strained. A teaspoonful of lemon-juice, some cayenne, and minced parsley should be added to it, and a little arrowroot, or flour and butter.

½ to ¾ hour.


## FRICASSEED FOWLS OR CHICKENS
### (*Entrée*)

To make a fricassee of good appearance without great expense, prepare, with exceeding nicety, a couple of plump chickens, strip off the skin, and carve them very neatly. Reserve the wings, breasts, merrythoughts, and thighs; and stew down the inferior joints with a couple of blades of mace, a small bunch of savoury herbs, a few white peppercorns, a pint and a half of water, and a small half-teaspoonful of salt. When something more than a third part reduced, strain the gravy, let it cool, and skim off every particle of fat. Arrange the joints which are to be fricasseed in one layer if it can be done conveniently, and pour to them as much of the gravy as will nearly cover them; add the very thin rind of half a fine fresh lemon, and simmer the fowls gently from half to three-quarters of an hour; throw in sufficient salt, pounded mace, and cayenne, to give the sauce a good flavour, thicken it with a large teaspoonful of arrowroot, and stir to it the third of a pint of rich boiling cream; then lift the stewpan from the fire, and shake it briskly round while the beaten yolks of three fresh eggs, mixed with a spoonful or two of cream, are added; continue to shake the pan gently above the fire till the sauce is just set, but it must not be allowed to boil, or it will curdle in an instant.

½ to ¾ hour.

## FRIED CHICKEN À LA MALABAR
### (*Entrée*)

This is an Indian dish. Cut up the chicken, wipe it dry, and rub it well with currie-powder mixed with a little salt; fry it in a bit of butter, taking care that it is of a nice light brown. In the mean time cut two or three onions into thin slices, draw them out into rings, and cut the rings into little bits about half an inch long; fry them for a long time gently in a little clarified butter, until they have gradually dried up and are of a delicate yellow-brown. Be careful that they are not burnt, as the burnt taste of a single bit would spoil the flavour of the whole. When they are as dry as chips, without the least grease or moisture upon them, mix a little salt with them, strew them over the fried chicken, and serve up with lemon on a plate.

We have extracted this recipe from a clever little work called the 'Hand-Book of Cookery'.

## TO ROAST A HAUNCH OF VENISON

To give venison the flavour and the tenderness so much prized by epicures, it must be well kept; and by taking the necessary precautions, it will hang a considerable time without detriment. Wipe it with soft dry cloths, wherever the slightest moisture appears on the surface, and dust it plentifully with freshly-ground pepper or powdered ginger, to preserve it from the flies. The application of the pyroligneous or acetic acid would effectually protect it from these, as well as from the effects of the weather; but the joint must then be, not only well washed, but *soaked* for some considerable time, and this would be very detrimental.

To prepare the venison for the spit, wash it slightly with tepid water or merely wipe it thoroughly with damp cloths, and dry it afterwards with clean ones; then lay over the fat side a large sheet of thickly-buttered paper, and next a paste of flour and water about three-quarters of an inch thick; cover this again with two or three sheets of stout paper, secure the whole well with twine, and lay the haunch to a sound clear fire; baste the paper immediately with butter or clarified dripping, and roast the joint from three hours and a half to four and a half, according to its weight and quality. Doe venison will require half an hour less time than buck venison. Twenty minutes before the joint is done remove the paste and paper, baste the meat in every part with butter, and dredge it very lightly with flour; let it take a pale brown colour, and send it to table as hot as possible with gravy in a tureen, and good currant jelly. It is not now customary to serve any other sauces with it.

3½ to 4½ hours.

*Obs.* The kind of gravy appropriate to venison is a matter on which individual taste must decide. When preparations of high savour are preferred to the pure flavour of the game, *Espagnole* (or Spanish sauce) can be sent to table with it. When a simple unflavoured one is better liked, some mutton cutlets freed entirely from fat, then very slightly broiled over a quick fire, and stewed gently down in a light extract of mutton prepared by Liebig's directions, Chapter 1, for about an hour, will produce an excellent plain gravy: it should be seasoned with salt and pepper (or fine cayenne) only. When venison abounds, it should be used for the gravy instead of mutton.

## TO ROAST A HARE
### (*In season from September to the 1st of March*)

After the hare has been skinned, or cased,* as it is called, wash it very thoroughly in cold water, and afterwards in warm. If in any degree overkept, or musty in the inside, which it will sometimes be when emptied before it is hung up and neglected afterwards, use vinegar, or the pyroligneous acid, well diluted, to render it sweet; then again throw it into abundance of water, that it may retain no taste of the acid. Pierce with the point of a knife any parts in which the blood appears to have settled, and

* [*'Casing' or skinning a hare seems to have been the origin of the phrase 'First catch your hare', attributed to Mrs Glasse.*]

soak them in tepid water, that it may be well drawn out. Wipe the hare dry, fill it with forcemeat, sew it up, truss and spit it firmly, baste it for ten minutes with lukewarm water mixed with a very little salt; throw this away, and put into the pan a quart or more of new milk; keep it constantly laded over the hare until it is nearly dried up, then add a large lump of butter, flour the hare, and continue the basting steadily until it is well browned; for unless this be done, and the roast be kept at a proper distance from the fire, the outside will become so dry and hard as to be quite uneatable. Serve the hare when done, with good brown gravy (of which a little should be poured round it in the dish), and with fine red currant jelly. This is an approved English method of dressing it, but we would recommend in preference, that it should be basted plentifully with butter from the beginning (the strict economist may substitute clarified beef-dripping, or marrow, and finish with a small quantity of butter only); and that the salt and water should be altogether omitted. First-rate cooks merely wipe the hare inside and out, and rub it with its own blood before it is laid to the fire, but there is generally a rankness about it, especially after it has been many days killed, which, we should say, renders the washing indispensable, unless a coarse game-flavour is liked.

1¼ to 1¾ hour.


## TO ROAST A PHEASANT

(In season from the beginning of October to the end of January. The licensed term of pheasant shooting commences on the 1st of October, and terminates on the 2nd of February, but as the birds will remain perfectly good in cold weather for two or three weeks, if from that time hung in a well-ventilated larder, they continue, correctly speaking, in season so long as they can be preserved fit for table after the regular market for them is closed: the same rule applies equally to other varieties of game.)

Unless kept to the proper point, a pheasant is one of the most tough, dry, and flavourless birds that is sent to table; but when it has hung as many days as it can without becoming really tainted, and is well roasted and served, it is most excellent eating. Pluck off the feathers carefully, cut a slit in the back of the neck to remove the crop, then draw the bird in the usual way, and either wipe the inside very clean with a damp cloth, or pour water through it; wipe the outside also, but with a dry cloth; cut off the toes, turn the head of the bird *under* the wing, with the bill laid straight along the breast, skewer the legs, which must not be crossed, flour the pheasant well, lay it to a brisk fire, and baste it constantly and plentifully with well flavoured butter. Send bread-sauce and good brown gravy to table with it. When a brace is served, one is sometimes larded, and the other not; but a much handsomer appearance is given to the dish by larding both. About three-quarters of an hour will roast them.

¾ hour; a few minutes less, if liked very much underdone; five or ten more for *thorough* roasting, with a *good* fire in both cases.

## BOUDIN OF PHEASANT
## À LA RICHELIEU
### (*Entrée*)

Take, quite clear from the bones, and from all skin and
sinew, the flesh of a half-roasted pheasant; mince, and
then pound it to the smoothest paste; add an equal bulk
of the floury part of some fine roasted potatoes, or of such
as have been boiled by Captain Kater's receipt [see p. 65],
and beat them together until they are well blended; next
throw into the mortar something less (in volume) of fresh
butter than there was of the pheasant-flesh, with a high
seasoning of mace, nutmeg, and cayenne, and a half-
teaspoonful or more of salt; pound the mixture afresh for
ten minutes or a quarter of an hour, keeping it turned
from the sides of the mortar into the middle; then add one
by one, after merely taking out the germs with the point
of a fork, two whole eggs and a yolk or two without the
whites, if these last will not render the mixture too moist.
Mould it into the form of a roll, lay it into a stewpan
rubbed with butter, pour boiling water on it and poach it
gently from ten to fifteen minutes. Lift it out with care,
drain it on a sieve, and when it is quite cold cover it
equally with beaten egg, and then with the finest bread-
crumbs, and broil it over a clear fire, or fry it in butter of
a clear golden brown. A good gravy should be made of the
remains of the bird and sent to table with it; the flavour
may be heightened with ham and eschalots, and small
mushrooms, sliced sideways, and stewed quite tender in
butter, may be mixed with the *boudin* after it is taken from

the mortar; or their flavour may be given more delicately by adding to it only the butter in which they have been simmered, well pressed from them through a strainer. The mixture, which should be set into a very cool place before it is moulded, may be made into several small rolls, which will require four or five minutes' poaching only. The flesh of partridges will answer quite as well as that of pheasants for this dish.

## PARTRIDGES WITH MUSHROOMS

For a brace of young well-kept birds, prepare from half to three-quarters of a pint of mushroom-buttons, or very small flaps [*flat mushrooms*], as for pickling. Dissolve over a gentle fire an ounce and a half of butter, throw in the mushrooms with a slight sprinkling of salt and cayenne, simmer them from eight to ten minutes, and turn them with the butter on to a plate; when they are quite cold, put the whole into the bodies of the partridges, sew them up, truss them securely, and roast them on a vertical jack with the heads downwards; or should an ordinary spit be used, tie them firmly to it, instead of passing it through them. Roast them the usual time, and serve them with brown mushroom sauce, or with gravy and bread sauce only. The birds may be trussed like boiled fowls, floured, and stewed slowly for thirty minutes; then turned, and simmered for another half hour with the addition of some mushrooms to the gravy; or they may be covered with small mushrooms stewed apart, when they are sent to table. They can also be served with their sauce only, simply thickened with a small quantity of fresh butter, smoothly mixed with less than a teaspoonful of arrowroot and flavoured with cayenne and a little catsup, wine, or store sauce.

Partridges, 2; mushrooms, ½ to ¾ pint; butter, 1½ oz; little mace and cayenne: roasted 30 to 40 minutes, or stewed 1 hour.

*Obs.* Nothing can be finer than the game flavour imbibed by the mushrooms with which the birds are filled, in this receipt.

## TO ROAST WILD DUCKS

A bit of soft bread soaked in port wine, or in claret, is sometimes put into them, but nothing more. Flour them well, lay them rather near to a very clear and brisk fire, that they may be quickly browned, and yet retain their juices. Baste them plentifully and constantly with butter, and, if it can be so regulated, let the spit turn with them rapidly. From fifteen to twenty minutes will roast them sufficiently for the generality of eaters; but for those who object to them much underdressed, a few additional minutes must be allowed. Something less of time will suffice when they are prepared for persons who like them scarcely more than heated through.

Teal, which is a more delicate kind of wild-fowl, is roasted in the same way: in from ten to fifteen minutes it will be enough done for the fashionable mode of serving it, and twenty minutes will dress it *well* at a good fire.

# Potted Meats, and Curries

## REMARKS ON CURRIES

The great superiority of the oriental curries over those generally prepared in England is not, we believe, altogether the result of a want of skill or of experience on the part of our cooks, but is attributable in some measure to many of the ingredients, which in a *fresh and green state* add so much to their excellence, being here beyond our reach.

With us, turmeric and cayenne pepper prevail in them often far too powerfully: the prodigal use of the former should be especially avoided, as it injures both the quality and the *colour* of the currie, which ought to be of a dark green, rather than of a red or yellow hue. A couple of ounces of a sweet, sound cocoa-nut, lightly grated and stewed for nearly or quite an hour in the gravy of a currie, is a great improvement to its flavour: it will be found particularly agreeable with that of sweetbreads, and may be served in the currie, or strained from it at pleasure. Great care, however, should be taken not to use, for the purpose, a nut that is rancid. Spinage, cucumber, vegetable marrow, tomatas, acid apples, green gooseberries (seeded), and tamarinds imported *in the shell* – not preserved – may all, in their season, be added, with very good effect, to curries of different kinds.

Potatoes and celery are also occasionally boiled down in them.

The rice for a currie should always be sent to table in a separate dish from it, and in serving them, it should be first helped, and the currie laid upon it.

## MR ARNOTT'S CURRIE-POWDER

> Turmeric, eight ounces.
> Coriander seed, four ounces.
> Cummin seed, two ounces.
> Foenugreek seed, two ounces.
> Cayenne, half an ounce.
> (More or less of this last to taste.)

Let the seeds be of the finest quality. Dry them well, pound, and sift them separately through a lawn sieve, then weigh, and mix them in the above proportions. This is an exceedingly agreeable and aromatic powder, when all the ingredients are perfectly fresh and good, but the preparing is rather a troublesome process. Mr Arnott recommends that when it is considered so, a 'high-caste' chemist should be applied to for it.

## MR ARNOTT'S CURRIE

'Take the heart of a cabbage, and nothing but the heart, that is to say, pull away all the outside leaves until it is about the size of an egg; chop it fine, add to it a couple of apples sliced thin, the juice of one lemon, half a teaspoonful of black pepper, with one large tablespoon-ful of *my* currie-powder, and mix the whole well together. Now take six onions that have been chopped fine and fried brown, a garlic head, the size of a nutmeg, also minced fine, two ounces of fresh butter, two table-spoonsful of flour, and one pint of strong mutton or beef gravy; and when these articles are boiling, add the for-mer ingredients, and let the whole be well stewed up together: if not hot enough, add cayenne pepper. Next put in a fowl that has been roasted and nicely cut up; or a rabbit; or some lean chops of pork or mutton; or a lob-ster, or the remains of yesterday's calf's head; or anything else you may fancy; and you will have an excellent cur-rie, fit for kings to partake of.

'Well! now for the rice! It should be put into water which should be frequently changed, and should remain in for half an hour at least; this both clears and soaks it. Have your saucepan full of water (the larger the better), and when it boils rapidly, throw the rice into it: it will be done in fifteen minutes. Strain it into a dish, wipe the saucepan dry, return the drained rice into it, and put it over a gentle fire for a few minutes, with a cloth over it: every grain will be separate. When served, do not cover the dish.'

*Obs.* We have already given testimony to the excel-lence of Mr Arnott's currie-powder, but we think the currie itself will be found somewhat too acid for English taste in general, and the proportion of onion and garlic by one half too much for any but well seasoned Anglo-Indian palates.

## A BENGAL CURRIE

Slice and fry three large onions in two ounces of butter, and lift them out of the pan when done. Put into a stewpan three other large onions and a small clove of garlic which have been pounded together, and smoothly mixed with a dessertspoonful of the best pale turmeric, a teaspoonful of powdered ginger, one of salt, and one of cayenne pepper; add to these the butter in which the onions were fried, and half a cupful of good gravy; let them stew for about ten minutes, taking care that they shall not burn. Next, stir to them the fried onions and half a pint more gravy; add a pound and a half of mutton, or of any other meat, free from bone and fat, and simmer it gently for an hour, or more should it not then be perfectly tender.

Fried onions, 3 large; butter, 2 oz; onions pounded, 3 large; garlic, 1 clove; turmeric, 1 dessertspoonful; powdered ginger, salt, cayenne, each 1 teaspoonful; gravy, ½ cupful: 10 minutes. Gravy, ½ pint; meat, 1½ lb: 1 hour or more.

## POTTED MEATS

Any tender and well-roasted meat, taken free of fat, skin, and gristle, as well as from the dry outsides, will answer for potting admirably, better indeed than that which is generally baked for the purpose, and which is usually quite deprived of its juices by the process. Spiced or *corned* beef also is excellent when thus prepared; and any of these will remain good a long time if mixed with cold fresh butter, instead of that which is clarified; but no addition that can be made to it will render the meat eatable, unless it be *thoroughly pounded*; reduced, in fact, to the smoothest possible paste, free from a single lump or a morsel of unbroken fibre. If *rent* into fragments, instead of being quite cut through the grain in being minced, before it is put into the mortar, no beating will bring it to the proper state. Unless it be *very* dry, it is better to pound it for some time before any butter is added, and it must be long and patiently beaten after all the ingredients are mixed, that the whole may be equally blended and well mellowed in flavour.

The quantity of butter required will depend upon the nature of the meat; ham and salted beef will need a larger proportion than roast meat, or than the breasts of poultry and game; white fish, from being less dry, will require comparatively little. Salmon, lobsters, prawns, and shrimps are all extremely good, prepared in this way. They should, however, be perfectly fresh when they are pounded, and be set immediately afterwards into a very cool place. For these, and for white meats in general, mace, nutmeg, and cayenne or white pepper, are the appropriate spices. A small quantity of cloves may be added to hare and other brown meat, but allspice we would not recommend unless the taste is known to be in favour of it.

## POTTED CHICKEN, PARTRIDGE, OR PHEASANT

Roast the birds as for table, but let them be thoroughly done, for if the gravy be left in, the meat will not keep half so well. Raise the flesh of the breast, wings, and merrythought, quite clear from the bones, take off the skin, mince, and then pound it very smoothly with about one third of its weight of fresh butter, or something less, if the meat should appear of a proper consistence without the full quantity; season it with salt, mace, and cayenne, only, and add these in small portions until the meat is rather highly flavoured with both the last; proceed with it as with other potted meats.

# 'The Eyes Should Always be Bright' . . . of Fish

## TO CHOOSE FISH

The cook should be well acquainted with the signs of freshness and good condition in fish, as they are most unwholesome articles of food when stale, and many of them are also dangerous eating when they are out of season. The eyes should always be bright, the gills of a fine clear red, the body stiff, the flesh firm, yet elastic to the touch, and the smell not disagreeable. When all these marks are reversed, and the eyes are sunken, the gills very dark in hue, the fish itself flabby and of offensive odour, it is bad, and should be avoided. The chloride of soda, will, it is true, restore it to a tolerably eatable state,* if it be not very much over-kept, but it will never resemble in quality and wholesomeness fish which is fresh from the water.

A good turbot is thick and full fleshed, and the under side is of a pale cream colour or yellowish white; when this is of a bluish tint, and the fish is thin and soft, it

---

* We have known this applied very successfully to salmon which from some hours' keeping in sultry weather had acquired a slight degree of taint, of which no trace remained after it was dressed; as a general rule, however, fish which is not *wholesomely fresh* should be rejected for the table.

should be rejected. The same observations apply equally to soles.

The best salmon and cod fish are known by a small head, very thick shoulders, and small tail; the scales of the former should be bright, and its flesh of a fine red colour; to be eaten in perfection it should be dressed as soon as it is caught, before the curd (or white substance which lies between the flakes of flesh) has melted and rendered the fish oily. In that state it is really crimp,* but continues so only for a very few hours; and it bears therefore a much higher price in the London market then, than when mellowed by having been kept a day or two.

The flesh of cod fish should be white and clear before it is boiled, white still after it is boiled, and firm though tender, sweet and mild in flavour, and separated easily into large flakes. Many persons consider it rather improved than otherwise by having a little salt rubbed along the inside of the backbone and letting it lie from twenty-four to forty-eight hours before it is dressed. It is sometimes served crimp like salmon, and must then be sliced as soon as it is dead, or within the shortest possible time afterwards.

Herrings, mackerel, and whitings, unless newly caught, are quite uneatable. When they are in good condition their natural colours will be very distinct and their whole appearance glossy and fresh. The herring when first taken from the water is of a silvery brightness; the back of the

* ['Crimp' fish is very fresh, and 'crimped' slices are slashed at the edges to make them cook more crisply.]

mackerel is of a bright green marked with dark stripes; but this becomes of a coppery colour as the fish grows stale. The whiting is of a pale brown or fawn colour with a pinkish tint; but appears dim and leaden-hued when no longer fresh.

Eels should be alive and brisk in movement when they are purchased, but the 'horrid barbarity,' as it is truly designated, of skinning and dividing them while they are so, is without excuse, as they are easily destroyed 'by piercing the spinal marrow close to the back part of the skull with a sharp pointed knife or skewer. If this is done in the right place all motion will instantly cease'. We quote Dr Kitchener's assertion on this subject; but we know that the mode of destruction which he recommends is commonly practised by the London fishmongers. Boiling water also will immediately cause vitality to cease, and is perhaps the most humane and ready method of destroying the fish.

Lobsters, prawns, and shrimps, are very stiff when freshly boiled, and the tails turn strongly inwards; when these relax, and the fish are soft and watery, they are stale; and the smell will detect their being so, instantly, even if no other symptoms of it be remarked. If bought alive, lobsters should be chosen by their weight and 'liveliness'. The hen lobster is preferred for sauce and soups, on account of the coral; but the flesh of the male is generally considered of fine flavour for eating. The vivacity of their leaps will show when prawns and shrimps are fresh from the sea.

Oysters should close forcibly on the knife when they are opened: if the shells are apart ever so little they are losing their condition, and when they remain far open the fish are dead and fit only to be thrown away. Small plump natives are very preferable to the larger and coarser kinds.

## THE MODE OF COOKING BEST ADAPTED TO DIFFERENT KINDS OF FISH

It is not possible, the reader will easily believe, to insert in a work of the size of the present volume, all the modes of dressing the many varieties of fish which are suited to our tables; we give, therefore, only the more essential receipts in detail, and add to them such general information as may, we trust, enable even a moderately intelligent cook to serve all that may usually be required, without difficulty.

There is no better way of dressing a good turbot, brill, John Dory, or cod's head and shoulders, than plain but careful boiling. Salmon is excellent in almost every mode in which it can be cooked or used. Boiled entire or in crimped slices; roasted in a cradle-spit or Dutch oven; baked; fried in small collops; collared; potted; dried and smoked; pickled or soused (this is the coarsest and least to be recommended process for it, of any); made into a raised or common pie, or a potato-pastry; served cold in or with savoury jelly, or with a *Mayonnaise* sauce; or laid on potatoes and baked, as in Ireland, it will be found GOOD.

Soles may be either boiled, or baked, or fried entire, or in fillets; curried; stewed in cream; or prepared by any of the directions given for them in the body of this chapter.

Plaice, unless when in full season and very fresh, is apt to be watery and insipid; but taken in its perfection and carefully cooked, it is very sweet and delicate in flavour. If large, it may be boiled with advantage either whole or in fillets; but to many tastes it is very superior when filleted, dipped into egg and bread-crumbs, and fried. The flesh may also be curried; or the plaice may be converted into water-souchy, or *soupe-maigre*: when small it is often fried whole.

Red mullet should always be *baked*, *broiled*, or *roasted*: it should on no occasion be boiled.

Mackerel, when broiled *quite whole*, or freed from the bones, divided, egged, crumbed, and fried, is infinitely superior to the same fish cooked in the ordinary manner.

The whiting, when *very fresh* and in season, is always delicate and good; and of all fish is considered the best suited to invalids. Perhaps *quite* the most wholesome mode of preparing it for them, is to open it as little as possible when it is cleansed, to leave the skin on, to dry the fish well, and to broil it gently. It should be sent very hot to table, and will require no sauce: twenty minutes will usually be required to cook it, if of moderate size.

The haddock is sometimes very large. We have had it occasionally from our southern coast between two and three feet in length, and it was then remarkably good when simply boiled, even the day after it was caught, the white curd between the flakes of flesh being like that of extremely fresh salmon. As it is in full season in mid-winter, it can be sent to a distance without injury. It is a *very* firm fish when large and in season; but, as purchased commonly at inland markets, is often neither fine in size nor quality. *One* of the best modes of cooking it is, to take the flesh entire from the bones, to divide it, dip it into egg and bread-crumbs, mixed with savoury herbs finely minced, and a seasoning of salt and spice, and to fry it like soles.

## TO BAKE FISH

A gentle oven may be used with advantage, for cooking almost every kind of fish, as we have ascertained from our own observation; but it must be subjected to a mild degree of heat only. This penetrates the flesh gradually, and converts it into wholesome succulent food; whereas, a *hot oven* evaporates all the juices rapidly, and renders the fish hard and dry. When small, they should be wrapped in oiled or buttered paper before they are baked; and when filleted, or left in any other form, and placed in a deep dish with or without any liquid before they are put into the oven, a buttered paper should still be laid closely upon them to keep the surface moist. Large pieces of salmon, conger eel, and other fish of considerable size are sometimes in common cookery baked like meat over potatoes pared and halved.

## FAT FOR FRYING FISH

This, whether it be butter, lard, or oil should always be excellent in quality, for the finest fish will be rendered unfit for eating if it be fried in fat that is rancid. When good, and used in sufficient quantity, it will serve for the same purpose several times, if strained after each frying, and put carefully away in a clean pan, provided always that it has not been smoked nor burned in the using.

Lard renders fish more crisp than butter does; but fresh, pure olive-oil (*salad oil*, as it is commonly called in England) is the *best* ingredient which can be used for it, and as it will serve well for the same purpose, many times in succession, if strained and carefully stored as we have already stated, it is not in reality so expensive as might be supposed for this mode of cooking. There should always be an ample quantity of it (or of any other *friture*)* in the pan, as the fish should be nearly covered with it, at the least; and it should cease to bubble before either fish or meat is laid into it, or it will be too much absorbed by the flesh, and will impart neither sufficient firmness, nor sufficient colour.

## SMALL JOHN DORIES, BAKED
### (*Author's Receipt – Good*)

We have found these fish when they were too small to be worth cooking in the usual way, excellent when quite simply baked in the following manner, the flesh being remarkably sweet and tender, much more so than it becomes by frying or broiling. After they've been cleaned, dry them in a cloth, season the insides slightly with fine salt, dredge a little flour on the fish, and stick a few very small bits of butter on them, but only just sufficient to

---

* The French term for fat of all kinds used in frying.

prevent their becoming dry in the oven; lay them singly on a flat dish, and bake them very gently from fourteen to sixteen minutes. Serve them with the same sauce as baked soles.

When extremely fresh, as it usually is in the markets of the coast, fish thus simply dressed *au four* is preferable to that more elaborately prepared by adding various condiments to it after it is placed in a deep dish, and covering it with a thick layer of bread-crumbs, moistened with clarified butter.

The appearance of the John Dories is improved by taking off the heads, and cutting away not only the fins but the filaments of the back.

## SALMON PUDDING, TO BE SERVED HOT OR COLD
### (*A Scotch Receipt – Good*)

Pound or chop small, or rub through a sieve one pound of cold boiled salmon freed entirely from bone and skin; and blend it lightly but thoroughly with half a pound of fine bread-crumbs, a teaspoonful of essence of anchovies, a quarter-pint of cream, a seasoning of fine salt and cayenne, and four well whisked eggs. Press the mixture closely and evenly into a deep dish or mould, buttered in every part, and bake it for one hour in a moderate oven.

Salmon, 1 lb; bread-crumbs, ½ lb; essence of anchovies, 1 teaspoonful; cream, ¼ pint; eggs, 4; salt and cayenne: baked 1 hour.

## TO DRESS THE SEA BREAM

The sea bream, which is common in many of our markets, is not considered a fish of first-rate quality; but if well broiled or baked, it will afford a good, and generally a *cheap*, dish of excellent appearance, the bream being of handsome size and form. Open and cleanse it perfectly, but do not remove the scales; fold it in a dry cloth to absorb the moisture which hangs about it; lay it over a gentle fire, and broil it slowly, that the heat may gradually penetrate the flesh, which is thick. Should any cracks appear on the surface, dredge a little flour upon them. If of ordinary weight, the bream will require quite half an hour's broiling; it should be turned, of course, when partially done. Send plain melted butter and anchovy sauce to table with it. In carving it, remove the skin and scales, and serve only the flesh which lies beneath them, and which will be very white and succulent. A more usual and less troublesome mode of dressing the bream is to season the inside slightly with salt and pepper or cayenne, to dust a little more salt on the outside, spread a few bits of butter upon it, and send it to a gentle oven. It is sometimes filled with common veal-stuffing, and then requires to be rather longer baked; and it is often merely wrapped in a buttered paper, and placed in a moderate oven for twenty-five or thirty minutes.

# Sea Kale, Dandelion, Myriad Vegetables

## OBSERVATIONS ON VEGETABLES

The quality of vegetables depends much both on the soil in which they are grown, and on the degree of care bestowed upon their culture; but if produced in ever so great perfection, their excellence will be entirely destroyed if they be badly cooked.

With the exception of artichokes, which are said to be improved by two or three days' keeping, all the summer varieties should be dressed before their first freshness has in any degree passed off (for their flavour is never so fine as within a few hours of their being cut or gathered); but when this cannot be done, precaution should be taken to prevent their withering. The stalk-ends of asparagus, cucumbers, and vegetable-marrow, should be placed in from one to two inches of cold water; and all other kinds should be spread on a cool brick floor. When this has been neglected, they must be thrown into cold water, for some time before they are boiled, to recover them, though they will prove even then but very inferior eating.

Vegetables when not sufficiently cooked are known to be so exceedingly unwholesome and indigestible, that the custom of serving them *crisp*, which means, in reality, only half-boiled, should be altogether disregarded when health is considered of more importance than fashion; but they should not be allowed to remain in the water after they are quite done, or both their nutritive properties and their flavour will be lost, and their good appearance destroyed. Care should be taken to *drain them thoroughly* in a warm strainer, and to serve them very hot, with well-made sauces, if with any.

Only dried peas or beans, Jerusalem artichokes, and potatoes, are put at first into cold water. All others require plenty of fast-boiling water, which should be ready salted and skimmed before they are thrown into it.

## TO CLEAR VEGETABLES
## FROM INSECTS

Lay them for half an hour or more into a pan of strong brine, with the stalk ends uppermost; this will destroy the small snails and other insects which cluster in the leaves, and they will fall out and sink to the bottom. A pound and a half of salt to the gallon of water will answer for this purpose, and if strained daily it will last for some time.

## POTATOES
*(Remarks on their properties and importance)*

There is no vegetable commonly cultivated in this country, we venture to assert, which is comparable in value to the potato when it is of a good sort, has been grown in a suitable soil, and is properly cooked and served. It *must* be very nutritious, or it would not sustain the strength of thousands of people whose almost sole food it constitutes, and who, when they can procure a sufficient supply of it to satisfy fully the demands of hunger, are capable of accomplishing the heaviest daily labour. It may not be wise to depend for subsistence on a root of which the crop unhappily is so frequently in these days destroyed or greatly injured by disease, and for which it is so difficult to find a substitute that is equally cheap, wholesome and satisfying; but we can easily comprehend the predilection of an entire people for a tuber which combines, like the potato, the solidity almost of bread, with the healthful properties of various other fresh vegetables, without their acidity; and which can also be cooked and served in so many different forms. The wretched manner in which it is dressed in many English houses renders it comparatively valueless, and accounts in a measure for the prodigality with which it is thrown away when cold, even in seasons when its price is highest.

## TO BOIL POTATOES
### (*As in Ireland*)

Potatoes, to boil well together, should be all of the same sort, and as nearly equal in size as may be. Wash off the mould, and scrub them very clean with a hard brush, but neither scoop nor apply a knife to them in any way, even to clear the eyes.* Rinse them well, and arrange

---

* 'Because', in the words of our clever Irish correspondent, 'the water through these parts is then admitted into the very heart of the vegetable; and as the latent heat, after cooking, is not sufficient to throw it off, this renders the potatoes very unwholesome.'

them compactly in a saucepan, so that they may not lie loose in the water, and that a small quantity may suffice to cover them. Pour this in cold, and when it boils, throw in about a large teaspoonful of salt, to the quart, and simmer the potatoes until they are nearly done, but for the last two or three minutes let them boil rapidly. When they are tender quite through, which may be known by probing them with a fork, pour all the water from them immediately, lift the lid of the saucepan to allow the steam to escape, and place them on a trivet, high over the fire, or by the side of it, until the moisture has entirely evaporated; then peel, and send them to table as quickly as possible, either in a hot napkin, or in a dish, of which the cover is so placed that the steam can pass off. There should be no delay in serving them after they are once taken from the fire. Irish families always prefer them served in their skins. Some kinds will be sufficiently boiled in twenty minutes, others in not less than three quarters of an hour.

20 minutes to 1 hour, or more.

*Obs.* The water in which they are boiled should barely cover the potatoes. After it is poured off, they should be steamed for twenty minutes or *half an hour*, if large.

*Obs.* 2. Habitual potato-eaters know well that this vegetable is never so good as when served in *the skin* the instant it is taken from the fire, dished in a hot napkin, or sent to table without a cover over it. It should also be clean and dry that it may at pleasure be taken in the fingers and broken like bread, or held in the dinner napkin while the inside is scooped out with the fork, thus forming it into a sort of cup.

## TO BOIL POTATOES
### (*The Lancashire Way*)

Pare the potatoes, cover them with cold water, and boil them slowly until they are quite tender, but watch them carefully, that they may not be overdone; drain off the water entirely, strew some salt over them, leave the saucepan uncovered by the side of the fire, and shake it forcibly every minute or two, until the whole of the potatoes appear dry and floury. Lancashire cooks dress the vegetable in this way to perfection, but it is far from an economical mode, as a large portion of the potato adheres to the saucepan; it has, however, many admirers.

## TO BOIL POTATOES
### (*Captain Kater's Receipt*)

Wash, wipe, and pare the potatoes, cover them with cold water, and boil them gently until they are done, pour off the water, and sprinkle a little fine salt over them; then take each potato separately with a spoon, and lay it into a clean *warm* cloth, twist this so as to press all the moisture from the vegetable, and render it quite round; turn it carefully into a dish placed before the fire, throw a cloth over, and when all are done, send them to table quickly. Potatoes dressed in this way are mashed without the slightest trouble; it is also by far the best method of preparing them for puddings or for cakes.

## CRISPED POTATOES, OR
## POTATO-RIBBONS
### (*Entremets – Or to serve with Cheese*)

Wash well, and wipe, some potatoes of good flavour; cut them up into slices of from half to a whole inch thick, free them from the skins, and then pare them round and round in very thin, and very long ribbons. Lay them into a pan of cold water, and half an hour before they are wanted for table lift them on to a sieve that they may be well drained. Fry them in good butter, which should be very hot when they are thrown in, until they are quite crisp, and lightly browned; drain and dry them on a soft cloth, pile them in a hot dish, strew over them a mixed seasoning of salt and cayenne in fine powder, and serve them without delay. For the second course, dress them in the same manner, but omit the cayenne. Five or six minutes will fry them.

## POTATO BOULETTES
### (*Entremets – Good*)

Boil some good potatoes as dry as possible; mash a pound of them very smoothly, and mix with them while they are still warm, two ounces of fresh butter, a teaspoonful of salt, a little nutmeg, the beaten and strained yolks of four eggs, and last of all the white thoroughly whisked. Mould the mixture with a teaspoon and drop it into a small pan of boiling butter, or of very pure lard, and fry the *boulettes* for five minutes over a moderate fire: they should be of a fine pale brown, and very light. Drain them well and dish them on a hot napkin.

Potatoes, 1 lb; butter, 2 oz; salt, 1 teaspoonful; eggs, 4: 5 minutes.

*Obs.* These *boulettes* are exceedingly light and delicate, and make an excellent dish for the second course; but we think that a few spoonsful of sweet fresh cream boiled with them until the mixture becomes dry, would both enrich them and improve their flavour. They should be dropped into the pan with the teaspoon, as they ought to be small, and they will swell in the cooking.

## POTATO RISSOLES
### (French)

Mash and season the potatoes with salt, and white pepper or cayenne, and mix them with plenty of minced parsley, and a small quantity of green onions, or eschalots; add sufficient yolks of eggs to bind the mixture together, roll it into small balls, and fry them in plenty of lard or butter over a moderate fire, or they will be too much browned before they are done through. Ham, or any other kind of meat finely minced, may be substituted for the herbs, or added to them.

## TO BOIL SEA-KALE

Wash, trim, and tie the kale in bunches, and throw it into plenty of boiling water with some salt in it. When it is perfectly tender, lift it out, drain it well from the water, and send it to table with good melted butter. When fashion is not particularly regarded we would recommend its being served upon a toast like asparagus. About twenty minutes will boil it, rather less for persons who like it crisp.

18 to 20 minutes.

## TO DRESS DANDELIONS LIKE SPINACH, OR AS A SALAD
### (*Very wholesome*)

This common weed of the fields and highways is an excellent vegetable, the young leaves forming an admirable adjunct to a salad, and much resembling endive when boiled and prepared in the same way, or in any of the modes directed for spinach. The slight bitterness of its flavour is to many persons very agreeable; and it is often served at well-appointed tables. It has also, we believe, the advantage of possessing valuable medicinal qualities. Take the roots before the blossom is at all advanced, if they can readily be found in that state; if not, pluck off and use the young leaves only. Wash them as clean as possible, and boil them tender in a large quantity of water salted as for sprouts or spinach. Drain them well, press them dry with a wooden spoon, and serve them quite plain with melted butter in a tureen; or, squeeze, chop, and heat them afresh, with a seasoning of salt and pepper, a *morsel* of butter rolled in flour, and a spoonful or two of gravy or cream. A very large portion of the leaves will be required for a dish, as they shrink exceedingly in the cooking. For a salad, take them very young and serve them entire, or break them quite small with the fingers; then wash and drain them. Dress them with oil and vinegar, or with any other sauce which may be preferred with them.

## ASPARAGUS POINTS DRESSED
## LIKE PEAS
### (*Entremets*)

This is a convenient mode of dressing asparagus, when it is too small and green to make a good appearance plainly boiled. Cut the points so far only as they are perfectly tender, in bits of equal size, not more than the third of an inch in length; wash them very clean, and throw them into plenty of boiling water, with the usual quantity of salt, and a *few* grains of carbonate of soda. When they are tolerably tender, which will be in from ten to twelve minutes, drain them well, and spread them on a clean cloth; fold it over them, wipe them gently, and when they are quite dry put them into a clean stewpan with a good slice of butter, which should be just dissolved before the asparagus is added; stew them in this over a brisk fire, shaking them often, for eight or ten minutes; dredge in about a small teaspoonful of flour, and add half that quantity of white sugar; then pour in boiling water to nearly cover the asparagus, and boil it rapidly until but little liquid remains: stir in the beaten yolks of two eggs, heap the asparagus high in a dish, and serve it very hot. The sauce should adhere entirely to the vegetable as in green peas *à la Française*.

## GREEN PEAS À LA FRANÇAISE, OR FRENCH FASHION
### (*Entremets*)

Throw a quart of young and freshly-shelled peas into plenty of spring water with a couple of ounces of butter, and with the hand work them together until the butter adheres well to the peas; lift them out, and drain them in a cullender; put them into a stewpan or thick saucepan without any water, and let them remain over a gentle fire, and be stirred occasionally for twenty minutes from the time of their first beginning to simmer; then pour to them as much boiling water as will just cover them; throw in a small quantity of salt, and keep them boiling quickly for forty minutes: stir well amongst them a small lump of sugar which has been dipped quickly into water, and a thickening of about half an ounce of butter very smoothly mixed with a teaspoonful of flour; shake them over the fire for two minutes, and serve them directly heaped high in a very hot dish. There will be no sauce except that which adheres to the peas if they be properly managed. We have found marrowfats excellent, dressed by this receipt. Fresh and good butter should be used with them always.

Peas, 1 quart; butter, 2 oz: 20 minutes. Water to cover the peas; little salt: 40 minutes. Sugar, small lump; butter, ½ oz; flour, 1 teaspoonful: 2 minutes.

## AN EXCELLENT RECEIPT FOR FRENCH BEANS À LA FRANÇAISE

Prepare as many young and freshly-gathered beans as will serve for a large dish, boil them tender, and drain the water well from them. Melt a couple of ounces of fresh butter, in a clean saucepan, and stir smoothly to it a small dessertspoonful of flour; keep these well shaken, and gently simmered until they are lightly browned, add salt and pepper, and pour to them by degrees a small cupful of good veal gravy (or, in lieu of this, of sweet rich cream), toss the beans in the sauce until they are as hot as possible; stir quickly in, as they are taken from the fire, the beaten yolks of two fresh eggs and a little lemon-juice, and serve them without delay. The eggs and lemon are sometimes omitted, and a tablespoonful of minced parsley is added to the butter and flour; but this, we think, is scarcely an improvement.

Beans, 1 to 2 quarts: boiled 15 to 20 minutes. Butter, 2 oz; flour, 1 dessertspoonful; salt and pepper; veal gravy, *small* cupful; yolks of eggs, 2; lemon-juice, a dessertspoonful.

## DRESSED CUCUMBERS

Pare and slice them very thin, strew a little fine salt over them, and when they have stood a few minutes, drain off the water, by raising one side of the dish, and letting it flow to the other; pour it away, strew more salt, and a moderate seasoning of pepper on them, add two or three tablespoonsful of the purest salad-oil, and turn the cucumbers well, that the whole may receive a portion of it; then pour over them from one to three dessertspoonsful of chili vinegar, and a little common, should it be needed; turn them into a clean dish and serve them.

*Obs.* If very young, cucumbers are usually dressed without being pared, but the tough rind of full-grown ones being extremely indigestible, should be avoided. The vegetable, though apt to disagree with persons of delicate habit, when sauced in the common English mode, with salt, pepper, and vinegar only, may often be eaten by them with impunity when dressed with plenty of oil. It is difficult to obtain this perfectly fresh and pure here; and hence, perhaps arises in part the prejudice which, amongst us, is so often found to exist against the use of this most wholesome condiment.

## CAULIFLOWERS À LA FRANÇAISE

Strip away all the green leaves, and divide each cauliflower into three or four parts, trimming the stalks quite close; put them, with the heads downwards, into a stewpan which will just hold them, half filled with boiling water, into which an ounce of good butter and some salt have previously been thrown; so soon as they are quite tender, drain the water from them, place a dish over the stewpan and turn it gently upside down; arrange the vegetables neatly in the form of one large cauliflower and cover it with good melted butter, into which a little lemon-juice has been stirred.

12 to 18 minutes.

## ROAST TOMATAS
(*To serve with roast leg, loin, or shoulder of mutton*)

Select them nearly of the same size, take off the stalks, and roast them gently in a Dutch oven, or if more convenient, place them at the edge of the dripping-pan, taking care that no fat from the joint shall fall upon them, and keeping them turned that they may be equally done. From ten to fourteen minutes will roast them.

## STEWED TOMATAS

Arrange them in a single layer, and pour to them as much gravy as will reach half their height; stew them very softly until the under sides are done, then turn, and finish stewing them. Thicken the gravy with a little arrowroot and cream, or with flour and butter, and serve it round them.

## FORCED [OR STUFFED] TOMATAS
(*English Receipt*)

Cut the stems quite close, slice off the tops of eight fine tomatas, and scoop out the insides; press the pulp through a sieve, and mix with it one ounce of fine crumbs of bread, one of butter broken very small, some pepper or cayenne, and salt. Fill the tomatas with the mixture and bake them for ten minutes in a moderate oven; serve them with brown gravy in the dish. A few small mushrooms stewed tender in a little butter, then minced and added to the tomata pulp, will very much improve this receipt.

Bake 10 minutes.

## MUSHROOMS AU BEURRE
### (*Delicious*)

Cut the stems from some fine meadow mushroom-buttons, and clean them with a bit of new flannel, and some fine salt; then either wipe them dry with a soft cloth, or rinse them in fresh water, drain them quickly, spread them in a clean cloth, fold it over them, and leave them for ten minutes, or more, to dry. For every pint of them thus prepared, put an ounce and a half of fresh butter into a thick iron saucepan, shake it over the fire until it *just* begins to brown, throw in the mushrooms, continue to shake the saucepan over a clear fire that they may not stick to it nor burn, and when they have simmered three or four minutes, strew over them a little salt, some cayenne, and pounded mace; stew them until they are perfectly tender, heap them in a dish, and serve them with their own sauce only, for breakfast, supper, or luncheon. Nothing can be finer than the flavour of the mushrooms thus prepared; and the addition of any liquid is far from an improvement to it. They are very good when drained from the butter, and served cold, and in a cool larder may be kept for several days. The butter in which they are stewed is admirable for flavouring gravies, sauces, or potted meats. Small flaps, freed from the fur and skin, may be stewed in the same way; and either these, or the buttons, served under roast poultry or partridges, will give a dish of very superior relish.

Meadow mushrooms, 3 pints; fresh butter, 4½ oz: 3 to 5 minutes. Salt, 1 small teaspoonful; mace, half as much; cayenne, third of saltspoonful: 10 to 15 minutes. More spices to be added if required – much depending on their quality; but they should not overpower the flavour of the mushrooms.

*Obs.* Persons inhabiting parts of the country where mushrooms are abundant, may send them easily, when thus prepared, to their friends in cities, or in less productive counties. If poured into jars, with sufficient butter to cover them, they will travel any distance, and can be re-warmed for use.

## TRUFFLES AND THEIR USES

The truffle, or underground mushroom, as it has sometimes been called, is held in almost extravagant estimation by epicures, and enters largely into what may be termed first-class cookery, both in England and abroad; though it is much less generally known and used here than in France, Germany, and other parts of the Continent, where it is far more abundant, and of very superior quality.

As it is in constant demand for luxuriously-served tables, and has hitherto, we believe, baffled all attempts to increase it by cultivation, it bears usually a high price in the English market, and is seldom to be had cheap in any; but although too costly for common consumption, where the expenditure is regulated by rational economy, it may at times be made to supply, at a reasonable expense, some excellent store-preparations for the breakfast and luncheon-table; as a small portion will impart its peculiar flavour to them.

The blackest truffles are considered the best. All are in their perfection during the latter part of November, December, and January; though they may be procured usually from October to March; yet as they are peculiarly subject to decay – or, properly speaking, become really putrid – from exposure to the air, it is an advantage to have them as early in their season as may be.

In sumptuous households the very finest foreign truffles are often served *as a vegetable* in the second course.


## TO BOIL SPROUTS, CABBAGES, SAVOYS, LETTUCES, OR ENDIVE

All green vegetables should be thrown into abundance of fast boiling water ready salted and skimmed, with the addition of the small quantity of carbonate of soda which we have recommended, in a previous page of this chapter [p. 69]; the pan should be left uncovered, and every precaution taken to prevent the smoke from reaching its contents. Endive, sprouts, and spring greens, will only require copious washing before they are boiled; but savoys, large lettuces, and close-leaved cabbages should be thrown into salt and water for half an hour or more before they are dressed, with the tops downwards to draw out the insects. The stems of these last should be cut off, the decayed leaves stripped away, and the vegetable halved or quartered, or split deeply across the stalk-end, and divided entirely before it is dished.

Very young greens, 15 to 20 minutes; lettuces, 20 to 30 minutes; large savoys, or cabbages, 1 to 1½ hour, or more.

*Obs.* When the stalk of any kind of cabbage is tender it is ready to serve. Turnip-greens should be well washed in several waters, and boiled in a very large quantity to deprive them of their bitterness.

## CARROTS
### (*Entrée – The Windsor Receipt*)

Select some good carrots of equal size, and cut the upper parts into even lengths of about two inches and a half, then trim one end of each into a point, so as to give the carrot the form of a sugar-loaf. When all are ready, throw them into plenty of ready-salted boiling water, and boil them three-quarters of an hour. Lift them out, and drain them well, then arrange them upright, and all on a level in a broad stewpan or saucepan, and pour in good hot beef-broth or veal gravy to half their height; add as much salt as may be needed, and a small teaspoonful of sugar, and boil them briskly for half an hour, or longer, should they require it. Place them again upright in dishing them, and keep them hot while a little good brown gravy is thickened to pour over them, and mixed with a large teaspoonful of parsley and a little lemon-juice; or sauce them with common *béchamel*, or white sauce, with or without the addition of parsley.

Thick part of carrots cut in cones: boiled ¾ hour. With gravy or broth, little salt and sugar: ½ hour, or more. Sauce: thickened gravy, *béchamel* made without meat, or common white sauce.

*Obs.* The carrots dressed thus are exceedingly good without any sauce beyond the small quantity of liquid which will remain in the stewpan with them, or with a few spoonsful more of gravy added to this, and thickened with butter and a little flour.

## CARROTS AU BEURRE, OR BUTTERED CARROTS
### (*French*)

Either boil sufficient carrots for a dish quite tender, and then cut them into slices a quarter of an inch thick, or first slice and then boil them: the latter method is the most expeditious, but the other best preserves the flavour of the vegetable. Drain them well, and while this is being done just dissolve from two to three ounces of butter in a saucepan, and strew in some minced parsley, some salt, and white pepper or cayenne; then add the carrots, and toss them very gently until they are equally covered with the sauce, which should not be allowed to boil: the parsley may be omitted at pleasure. Cold carrots may be re-warmed in this way.

## FRIED PARSNEPS

Boil them until they are about half done, lift them out, and let them cool; slice them rather thickly, sprinkle them with fine salt and white pepper, and fry them a pale brown in good butter. Serve them with roast meat, or dish them under it.

## JERUSALEM ARTICHOKES

Wash the artichokes, pare them quickly, and throw them as they are done into a saucepan of cold water, or of equal parts of milk and water; and when they are about half boiled add a little salt to them. Take them up the instant they are perfectly tender: this will be in from fifteen to twenty-five minutes, so much do they vary in size and as to the time necessary to dress them. If allowed to remain in the water after they are done, they become black and flavourless. Melted butter should always be sent to table with them.

15 to 25 minutes.

## TO BAKE BEET ROOT

Beet root if slowly and carefully baked until it is tender quite through, is very rich and sweet in flavour, although less bright in colour than when it is boiled: it is also, we believe, remarkably nutritious and wholesome. Wash and wipe it very dry, but neither cut nor break any part of it, then lay it into a coarse earthen dish, and bake it in a gentle oven for four or five hours: it will sometimes require even a longer time than this. Pare it quickly if it be served hot; but leave it to cool first, when it is to be sent to table cold.

In a slow oven from 4 to 6 hours.

## TO STEW RED CABBAGE
### (*Flemish Receipt*)

Strip the outer leaves from a fine and fresh red cabbage; wash it well, and cut it into the thinnest possible slices, beginning at the top; put it into a thick saucepan in which two or three ounces of good butter have been dissolved; add some pepper and salt, and stew it very slowly indeed for three or four hours in its own juice, keeping it often stirred, and well pressed down. When it is perfectly tender add a tablespoonful of vinegar; mix the whole up thoroughly, heap the cabbage in a hot dish, and serve broiled sausages round it; or omit these last, and substitute lemon-juice, cayenne pepper, and half a cupful of good gravy.

The stalk of the cabbage should be split in quarters and taken entirely out in the first instance.

3 to 4 hours.

## BRUSSELS SPROUTS

These delicate little sprouts, or miniature cabbages, which at their fullest growth scarcely exceed a large walnut in size, should be quite freshly gathered. Free them from all discoloured leaves, cut the stems even, and wash the sprouts thoroughly. Throw them into a pan of water properly salted, and boil them quickly from eight to ten minutes; drain them *well*, and serve them upon a rather thick round of toasted bread buttered on both sides. Send good melted butter to table with them. This is the Belgian mode of dressing this excellent vegetable, which is served in France with the sauce poured over it, or it is tossed in a stewpan with a slice of butter and some pepper and salt: a spoonful or two of veal gravy (and sometimes a little lemon-juice) is added when these are perfectly mixed.

8 to 10 minutes.

## SALSIFY

We are surprised that a vegetable so excellent as this should be so little cared for in England. Delicately fried in batter – which is a common mode of serving it abroad – it forms a delicious second course dish: it is also good when plain-boiled, drained, and served in gravy, or even with melted butter. Wash the roots, scrape gently off the dark outside skin, and throw them into cold water as they are done, to prevent their turning black; cut them into lengths of three or four inches, and when all are ready put them into plenty of boiling water with a little salt, a small bit of butter, and a couple of spoonsful of white vinegar or the juice of a lemon: they will be done in from three-quarters of an hour to an hour. Try them with a fork, and when perfectly tender, drain, and serve them with a white sauce, rich brown gravy, or melted butter.

¾ to 1 hour.

## STEWED ONIONS

Strip the outer skin from four to five fine Portugal onions, and trim the ends, but without cutting into the vegetable;

arrange them in a saucepan of sufficient size to contain them all in one layer; just cover them with good beef or veal gravy, and stew them very gently indeed for a couple of hours: they should be tender quite through, but should not be allowed to fall to pieces. When large, but not *mild* onions are used, they should be first boiled for half an hour in plenty of water, then drained from it, and put into boiling gravy: strong, well-flavoured broth of veal or beef, is sometimes substituted for this, and with the addition of a little catsup, spice, and thickening, answers very well. The savour of this dish is heightened by flouring lightly and frying the onions of a pale brown before they are stewed.

Portugal onions, 4 or 5 (if fried, 15 to 20 minutes); broth or gravy, 1 to 1½ pint: nearly or quite 2 hours.

*Obs.* When the quantity of gravy is considered too much, the onions may be only half covered, and turned when the under side is tender, but longer time must then be allowed for stewing them.

## STEWED CHESTNUTS

Strip the outer rind from forty or fifty fine sound Spanish chestnuts, throw them into a large saucepan of hot water, and bring it to the point of boiling; when the second skin parts from them easily, lift them out, and throw them into plenty of cold water; peel, and wipe them dry; then put them into a stewpan or bright saucepan, with as much highly-flavoured cold beef or veal gravy as will nearly cover them, and stew them very gently from three-quarters of an hour to a full hour: they should be quite tender, but unbroken. Add salt, cayenne, and thickening if required, and serve the chestnuts in their gravy. We have found it an improvement to have them floured and lightly browned in a little good butter before they are stewed, and also to add some thin strips of fresh lemon-rind to the gravy.

Chestnuts, 40 or 50; gravy, ¾ pint, or more: ¾ to 1 hour.

*Obs.* A couple of bay leaves and a slice of lean ham will give an improved flavour to the sauce should it not be sufficiently rich: the ham should be laid under the chestnuts, but not served with them. When these are to be browned, or even otherwise, they may be freed readily from the second skin by shaking them with a small bit of butter in a frying-pan over a gentle fire.

# Gravy in Haste and More Sauces

### BARON LIEBIG'S BEEF GRAVY
(*Most excellent for hashes, minces, and other
dishes made of cold meat*)

For particulars of this most useful receipt, for extracting
all its juices from fresh meat of every kind in the best
manner, the cook is referred to the first part of the chapter
on soups. The preparation, for which minute directions
are given there [p. 4] if poured on a few bits of lean ham
lightly browned, with the other ingredients indicated
above, will be converted into gravy of fine flavour and
superior quality.

With no addition, beyond that of a little thickening
and spice, it will serve admirably for dressing cold meat,
in all the usual forms of hashes, minces, *blanquettes*, etc.,
and convert it into dishes as nourishing as those of meat
freshly cooked, and it may be economically made in
small quantities with any trimmings of *undressed* beef,
mutton, or veal, mixed together, which are free from fat,
and not sinewy: flavour may be given to it at once by
chopping up with them the lean part only of a slice or
two of ham, or of highly-cured beef.

## ESPAGNOLE (SPANISH SAUCE)
### (*A highly-flavoured Gravy*)

Dissolve a couple of ounces of good butter in a thick stewpan or saucepan, throw in from four to six sliced eschalots, four ounces of the lean of an undressed ham, three ounces of carrot, cut in small dice, one bay leaf, two or three branches of parsley, and one or two of thyme, but these last must be small; three cloves, a blade of mace, and a dozen corns of pepper; add part of a root of parsley, if it be at hand, and keep the whole stirred or shaken over a moderate fire for twenty minutes, then add by degrees one pint of very strong veal stock or gravy, and stew the whole gently from thirty to forty minutes; strain it, skim off the fat, and it will be ready to serve.

Butter, 2 oz; eschalots, 4 to 6; lean of undressed ham 4 oz; carrots, 3 oz; bay leaf, 1; little thyme and parsley, in branches; cloves, 3; mace, 1 blade; peppercorns, 12; little parsley root: fried gently, 20 minutes. Strong veal stock, or gravy, 1 pint: stewed very softly, 30 to 40 minutes.

## GRAVY IN HASTE

Chop fine a few bits of lean meat, a small onion, a few slices of carrot and turnip, and a little thyme and parsley; put these with half an ounce of butter into a thick saucepan, and keep them stirred until they are slightly browned; add a little spice, and water in the proportion of a pint to a pound of meat; clear the gravy from scum, let it boil half an hour, then strain it for use.

Meat, 1 lb; 1 small onion; little carrot, turnip, thyme, and parsley; butter, ½ oz; cloves, 6; corns of pepper, 12; water, 1 pint: ½ hour.

## TO THICKEN SAUCES

When this is done with the yolks of eggs, they should first be well beaten, and then mixed with a spoonful of cold stock should it be at hand, and with one or two of the boiling sauce, which should be stirred very quickly to them, and they must in turn be stirred briskly to the sauce, which may be held over the fire, and well shaken for an instant afterwards, but never placed upon it, nor allowed to boil.

To the *roux* or French thickening, the gravy or other liquid which is to be mixed with it should be poured boiling and in small quantities, the saucepan being often well shaken round, and the sauce made to boil up after each portion is added. If this precaution be observed, the butter will never float upon the surface, but the whole will be well and smoothly blended: it will otherwise be difficult to clear the sauce from it perfectly.

For invalids, or persons who object to butter in their soups or sauces, flour only mixed to a smooth batter, and stirred into the boiling liquid may be substituted for other thickening: arrowroot also used in the same way, will answer even better than flour.

# SAUCE TOURNÉE, OR PALE THICKENED GRAVY

Sauce tournée is nothing more than rich pale gravy made with veal or poultry and thickened with delicate white *roux*. The French give it a flavouring of mushrooms and green onions, by boiling some of each in it for about half an hour before the sauce is served: it must then be strained, previously to being dished. Either first dissolve an ounce of butter, and then dredge gradually to it three-quarters of an ounce of flour, and proceed as for the preceding receipt; or blend the flour and butter perfectly with a knife before they are thrown into the stewpan, and keep them stirred without ceasing over a clear and gentle fire until they have simmered for some minutes, then place the stewpan high over the fire, and shake it constantly until the *roux* has lost the raw taste of the flour; next, stir very gradually to it a pint of the gravy, which should be boiling. Set it by the side of the stove for a few minutes, skim it thoroughly, and serve it without delay.

Butter, 1 oz; flour, ¾ oz; strong pale gravy, seasoned with mushrooms and green onions, 1 pint.

*Obs.* With the addition of three or four yolks of very fresh eggs, mixed with a seasoning of mace, cayenne, and lemon-juice, this becomes *German sauce*, now much used for fricassees, and other dishes; and minced parsley (boiled) and chili vinegar, each in sufficient quantity to flavour it agreeably, convert it into a good fish sauce.

# BÉCHAMEL

This is a fine French white sauce, now very much served at good English tables. It may be made in various ways, and more or less expensively; but it should always be thick, smooth, and rich, though delicate in flavour. The most ready mode of preparing it is to take an equal portion of very strong, pale veal gravy, and of good cream (a pint of each for example), and then, by rapid boiling over a very clear fire, to reduce the gravy nearly half; next, to mix with part of the cream a tablespoonful of fine dry flour, to pour it to the remainder, when it boils, and to keep the whole stirred for five minutes or more over a slow fire, for if placed upon a fierce one it would be liable to burn; then to add the gravy, to stir and mix the sauce perfectly, and to simmer it for a few minutes longer. All the flavour should be given by the gravy, in which French cooks boil a handful of mushrooms, a *few* green onions, and some branches of parsley before it is reduced: but a good *béchamel* may be made without them, with a strong *consommé* well reduced.

Strong pale veal gravy (flavoured with mushrooms or not), 1 pint: reduced half. Rich cream, 1 pint; flour, 1 tablespoonful: 5 minutes. With gravy, 4 or 5 minutes.

*Obs. Velouté*, which is a rather thinner sauce or gravy, is made by simply well reducing the cream and stock separately, and then mixing them together without any thickening.

## BÉCHAMEL MAIGRE
### (*A cheap White Sauce*)

A good *béchamel* may be made entirely without meat, when economy is an object, or when no gravy is at hand. Put into a stewpan, with from two to three ounces of butter, a carrot, and a couple of small onions, cut in slices, with a handful of nicely-cleaned mushroom buttons, when these last can be easily procured; and when they have stewed slowly for half an hour, or until the butter is nearly dried up, stir in two tablespoonsful of flour, and pour in a pint of new milk, a little at a time, shaking the stewpan well round, that the sauce may be smooth. Boil the *béchamel* gently for half an hour; add a little salt, and cayenne; strain, and reduce it, if not quite thick, or pour in boiling to the yolks of two fresh eggs.

## FRENCH MELTED BUTTER

Pour half-pint of good but not very thick, boiling melted butter to the well-beaten yolks of two or three fresh eggs, and stir them briskly as it is added; put the sauce again into the saucepan, and shake it high over the fire for an instant, but do not allow it to boil or it will curdle. Add a little lemon-juice or vinegar, and serve it immediately.

## NORFOLK SAUCE, OR RICH MELTED BUTTER WITHOUT FLOUR

Put three tablespoonsful of water into a small saucepan, and when it boils add four ounces of fresh butter; as soon as this is quite dissolved, take the saucepan from the fire, and shake it round until the sauce looks thick and smooth. It must not be allowed to boil after the butter is added.

Water, 3 tablespoonsful; butter, 4 oz.

## VERY GOOD EGG SAUCE

Boil four fresh eggs for quite fifteen minutes, then lay them into plenty of fresh water, and let them remain until they are perfectly cold. Break the shells by rolling them on a table, take them off, separate the white from the yolks, and divide all of the latter into quarter-inch dice; mince two of the white tolerably small, mix them lightly, and stir them into the third of a pint of rich melted butter or of white sauce: serve the whole as hot as possible.

Eggs, 4: boiled 15 minutes, left till cold. The yolks of all, whites of 2; third of pint of good melted butter or white sauce. Salt as needed.

## CREAM SAUCE FOR FISH

Knead very smoothly together with a strong-bladed knife, a *large* teaspoonful of flour with three ounces of good butter; stir them in a very clean saucepan or stew-pan over a gentle fire until the butter is dissolved, then throw in a little salt and some cayenne, give the whole one minute's simmer, and add, very gradually, half a pint of good cream; keep the sauce constantly stirred, until it boils, then mix with it a dessertspoonful of essence of anchovies, and half as much chili vinegar or lemon-juice. The addition of shelled shrimps or lobsters cut in dice, will convert this at once into a most excellent sauce of either. Pounded mace may be added to it with the cayenne: and it may be thinned with a few spoonsful of milk should it be too thick. Omit the essence of anchovies, and mix with it some parsley boiled very green and minced, and it becomes a good sauce for poultry.

Butter, 3 oz; flour, 1 *large* teaspoonful: 2 to 3 minutes. Cream, ½ pint; essence of anchovies, 1 large dessert-spoonful (more if liked); chili vinegar or lemon juice, 1 teaspoonful; salt, ¼ saltspoonful.


## SAUCE ROBERT

Cut four or five large onions into small dice, and brown them in a stewpan, with three ounces of butter and a dessertspoonful of flour. When of a deep yellow brown, pour to them half a pint of beef or of veal gravy, and let them simmer for fifteen minutes; skim the sauce, add a dessertspoonful of made mustard with it.

Large onions, 4 or 5; butter, 3 oz; flour, dessertspoon-ful: 10 to 15 minutes. Gravy, ½ pint: 15 minutes. Mustard, dessertspoonful.

## COMMON SAUCE OF CUCUMBERS

Cucumbers which have the fewest seeds are best for this sauce. Pare and slice *two* or *three*, should they be small, and put them into a saucepan, in which two ounces, or rather more, of butter have been dissolved, and are beginning to boil; place them high over the fire, that they may stew as softly as possible, without taking colour, for three-quarters of an hour, or longer should they require it; add to them a good seasoning of white pepper and some salt, when they are half done; and just before they are served stir to them half a teaspoonful of flour, mixed with a morsel of butter; strew in some minced parsley, give it a boil, and finish with a spoonful of good vinegar.

## SUPERIOR MINT-SAUCE
### (*To serve with lamb*)

The mint for this sauce should be fresh and young, for when old it is tough and indigestible. Strip the leaves from the stems, wash them with great nicety, and drain them on a sieve, or dry them in a cloth; chop them very fine, put them into a sauce-tureen, and to three heaped table-spoonsful of the mint add two of pounded sugar; let them remain a short time well mixed together, then pour to them gradually six tablespoonsful of good vinegar. The sauce thus made is excellent, and far more wholesome than when a larger proportion of vinegar and a smaller one of sugar is used for it; but, after the first trial, the proportions can easily be adapted to the taste of the eaters.

# Monitor's Tart and Other Pastry

## INTRODUCTORY REMARKS

The greatest possible cleanliness and nicety should be observed in making pastry. The slab or board, paste-rollers, tins, cutters, moulds, everything, in fact, used for it, and especially the hands, should be equally free from the slightest soil or particle of dust. The more expeditiously the finer kinds of paste are made and dispatched to the oven, and the less they are touched the better.

In mixing paste, the water should be added gradually, and the whole gently drawn together with the finger, until sufficient has been added, when it should be lightly kneaded until it is as smooth as possible. When carelessly made, the surface is often left covered with small dry crumbs or lumps; or the water is poured in heedlessly in so large a proportion that it becomes necessary to add more flour to render it *workable* in any way; and this ought particularly to be avoided when a certain weight of all the ingredients has been taken.

## ENGLISH PUFF PASTE

Break lightly into a couple of pounds of dried and sifted flour eight ounces of butter; add a pinch of salt, and sufficient cold water to make the paste; work it as quickly and as lightly as possible, until it is smooth and pliable, then level it with the paste-roller until it is three-quarters of an inch thick, and place regularly upon it six ounces of butter in small bits; fold the paste, roll it out again, lay on it six ounces more of butter, repeat the rolling, dusting each time a little flour over the board and paste, add again six ounces of butter, and roll the paste out thin three or four times, folding the ends into the middle.

Flour, 2 lb; little salt; butter, 1 lb 10 oz.

If very rich paste be required, equal portions of flour and butter must be used; and the latter may be divided into two, instead of three parts, when it is to be rolled in.


## CREAM CRUST
### (*Author's Receipt – Very good*)

Stir a little fine salt into a pound of dry flour, and mix gradually with it sufficient very thick, sweet cream to form a smooth paste; it will be found sufficiently good for common family dinners, without the addition of butter; but to make an excellent crust, roll in four ounces in the usual way, after having given the paste a couple of *turns*. Handle it as lightly as possible in making it, and send it to the oven as soon as it is ready: it may be used for fruit tarts, cannelons, puffs, and other varieties of small pastry, or for good meat pies. Six ounces of butter to the pound of flour will give a *very rich* crust.

Flour, 1 lb; salt, 1 small saltspoonful (more for meat pies); rich cream, ½ to ¾ pint; butter, 4 oz; for richest crust, 6 oz.

## VERY RICH SHORT CRUST FOR TARTS

Break lightly, with the least possible handling, six ounces of butter into eight of flour; add a dessertspoonful of pounded sugar, and two or three of water; roll the paste, for several minutes, to blend the ingredients well, folding it together like puff crust, and touch it as little as possible.

Flour, 8 oz; butter, 6 oz; pounded sugar, 1 dessertspoonful; water, 2 to 3 spoonsful.

## EXCELLENT SHORT CRUST
## FOR SWEET PASTRY

Crumble down very lightly half a pound of butter into a pound of flour, breaking it quite small. Mix well with these a slight pinch of salt and two ounces of sifted sugar, and add sufficient milk to make them up into a very smooth and somewhat firm paste. Bake this slowly, and keep it pale. It will be found an admirable crust if well made and lightly handled, and will answer for many dishes much better than puff paste. It will rise in the oven too, and be extremely light. Ten ounces of butter will render it very rich, but we find eight quite sufficient.

## MODERN CHICKEN PIE

Skin, and cut down into joints a couple of fowls, take out all the bones, and season the flesh highly with salt, cayenne, pounded mace, and nutmeg; line a dish with a thin paste, and spread over it a layer of the finest sausage-meat, which has previously been moistened with a spoonful or two of cold water; over this place closely together some of the boned chicken joints, then more sausage-meat, and continue thus with alternate layers of each, until the dish is full; roll out, and fasten securely at the edge, a cover half an inch thick, trim off the superfluous paste, make an incision in the top, lay some paste leaves round it, glaze the whole with yolk of egg, and bake the pie from an hour and a half to two hours in a well heated oven. Lay a sheet or two of writing-paper over the crust, should it brown too quickly. Minced herbs can be mixed with the sausage-meat at pleasure, and a small quantity of eschalot also, when its flavour is much liked: it should be well moistened with water, or the whole will be unpalatably dry. The pie may be served hot or cold, but we would rather recommend the latter.

A couple of very young tender rabbits will answer exceedingly well for it instead of fowls, and a border, or half paste in the dish will generally be preferred to an entire lining of the crust, which is now but rarely served, unless for pastry which is to be taken out of the dish or mould in which it is baked before it is sent to table.

## TOURTE MERINGUÉE, OR TART WITH ROYAL ICING

Lay a band of fine paste round the rim of a tart-dish, fill it with any kind of fruit mixed with a moderate proportion of sugar, roll out the cover very evenly, moisten the edges of the paste, press them together carefully, and trim them off close to the dish; spread equally over the top, to within rather more than an inch of the edge all round, the whites of three fresh eggs beaten to a quite solid froth and mixed quickly at the moment of using them with three tablespoonsful of dry sifted sugar. Put the tart into a moderately brisk oven, and when the crust has risen well and the icing is set, either lay a sheet of writing-paper lightly over it, or draw it to a part of the oven where it will not take too much colour. This is now a fashionable mode of icing tarts, and greatly improves their appearance.

Bake half an hour.

## SUPERLATIVE MINCEMEAT

Take four large lemons, with their weight of golden pippins pared and cored, of jar-raisins, currants, candied citron and orange-rind, and the finest suet, and a fourth part more of pounded sugar. Boil the lemons tender, chop them small, but be careful first to extract all the pips; add them to the other ingredients, after all have been prepared with great nicety, and mix the whole *well* with from three to four glasses of good brandy. We think that the weight of one lemon, in meat, improves this mixture; or, in lieu of it, a small quantity of crushed macaroons added just before it is baked.

## MINCE PIES
### (*Entremets*)

Butter some tin pattypans well, and line them evenly with fine puff paste rolled thin; fill them with mincemeat, moisten the edges of the covers, which should be nearly a quarter of an inch thick, close the pies carefully, trim off the superfluous paste, make a small aperture in the centre of the crust with a fork or the point of a knife, ice the pies or not, at pleasure, and bake them half an hour in a well-heated but not fierce oven: lay a paper over them when they are partially done, should they appear likely to take too much colour.

½ hour.

## MINCE PIES ROYAL
### (*Entremets*)

Add to half a pound of good mincemeat an ounce and a half of pounded sugar, the grated rind and the strained juice of a large lemon, one ounce of clarified butter, and the yolks of four eggs; beat these well together, and half fill, or rather more, with the mixture, some pattypans lined with fine paste; put them into a moderate oven and when the insides are just set, ice them thickly with the whites of the eggs beaten to snow, and mixed quickly at the moment with four heaped tablespoonsful of pounded sugar; set them immediately into the oven again, and bake them slowly of a fine light brown.

Mincemeat, ½ lb; sugar, 1½ oz; rind and juice, 1 large lemon; butter, 1 oz; yolks, 4 eggs. Icing: whites, 4 eggs; sugar, 4 tablespoonsful.

## THE MONITOR'S TART, OR TOURTE À LA JUDD

Put into an enamelled stewpan, or into a delicately clean saucepan, three-quarters of a pound of well-flavoured apples, weighed after they are pared and cored; add to them from three to four ounces of pounded sugar, an ounce and a half of fresh butter cut small, and half a teaspoonful of pounded cinnamon, or the lightly grated rind of a small lemon. Let them stand over, or by the side of a gentle fire until they begin to soften, and toss them now and then to mingle the whole well, but do not stir them with a spoon; they should all remain unbroken and rather firm. Turn them into a dish, and let them become cold. Divide three-quarters of a pound of good light paste into two equal portions; roll out one quite thin and round, flour an oven-leaf and lay it on, as the tart cannot so well be moved after it is made; place the apples upon it in the form of a dome, but leave a clear space of an inch or more round the edge; moisten this with white of egg, and press the remaining half of the paste (which should be rolled out to the same size, and laid carefully over the apples) closely upon it: they should be well secured, that the syrup from the fruit may not burst through. Whisk the white of an egg to a froth, brush it over the tart with a paste brush or a small bunch of feathers, sift sugar thickly over, and then strew upon it some almonds blanched and roughly chopped; bake the tart in a moderate oven from thirty-five to forty-five minutes. It may be filled with peaches, or apricots, half stewed like the apples, or with cherries merely rolled in fine sugar.

Light paste, ½ to ¾ lb; apples, 12 oz; butter, 1½ oz; sugar, 4 oz; glazing of egg and sugar; some almonds: 35 to 45 minutes.

## PUDDING PIES
### (*Entremets*)

This form of pastry (or its name at least) is, we believe, peculiar to the county of Kent, where it is made in abundance, and eaten by all classes of people during Lent. Boil for fifteen minutes three ounces of ground rice in a pint and a half of new milk, and when taken from the fire stir into it three ounces of butter and four of sugar; add to these six well-beaten eggs, a grain or two of salt, and a flavouring of nutmeg or lemon-rind at pleasure. When the mixture is nearly cold, line some large patty-pans or some saucers with thin puff paste, fill them with it three parts full, strew the tops thickly with currants which have been cleaned and dried, and bake the pudding pies from fifteen to twenty minutes in a gentle oven.

Milk, 1½ pint; ground rice, 3 oz: 15 minutes. Butter, 3 oz; sugar, ¼ lb; nutmeg or lemon-rind; eggs, 6; currants, 4 to 6 oz: 15 to 20 minutes.

## COMMON LEMON TARTLETS

Beat four eggs until they are exceedingly light, add to them gradually four ounces of pounded sugar, and whisk these together for five minutes; strew lightly in, if it be at hand, a dessertspoonful of potato-flour, if not, of common flour well dried and sifted, then throw into the mixture by slow degrees, three ounces of good butter, which should be dissolved, but only just luke-warm:

beat the whole well, then stir briskly in, the strained juice and the grated rind of one lemon and a half. Line some pattypans with fine puff paste rolled very thin, fill them two-thirds full, and bake the tartlets about twenty minutes, in a moderate oven.

Eggs, 4; sugar, 4 oz; potato-flour, or common flour, 1 dessertspoonful; butter, 3 oz; juice and rind of 1½ full-sized lemon: baked 15 to 20 minutes.

## APPEL KRAPFEN
### (*German Receipt*)

Boil down three-quarters of a pound of good apples with four ounces of pounded sugar, and a small glass of white wine, or the strained juice of a lemon; when they are stewed quite to a pulp, keep them stirred until they are thick and dry; then mix them gradually with four ounces of almonds, beaten to a paste, or very finely chopped, two ounces of candied orange or lemon-rind shred extremely small, and six ounces of jar raisins stoned and quartered: to these the Germans add a rather high flavouring of cinnamon, which is a very favourite spice with them, but a grating of nutmeg, and some fresh lemon-peel, are, we think, preferable for this composition. Mix all the ingredients well together; roll out some butter-crust a full back-of-knife thickness, cut it into four-inch squares, brush the edges to the depth of an inch round with beaten egg, fill them with the mixture, lay another square of paste on each, press them very securely together, make, with the point of a knife a small incision in the top of each, glaze them or not at pleasure, and bake them rather slowly, that the raisins may have time to become tender. They are very good. The proportion of sugar must be regulated by the nature of the fruit; and that of the almonds can be diminished when it is thought too much. A delicious tart of the kind is made by substituting for the raisins and candied orange-rind, two heaped tablespoonsful of very fine apricot jam.

# Soufflés and Omlets

## A FONDU, OR CHEESE SOUFFLÉ

Mix to a smooth batter, with a quarter-pint of new milk, two ounces of potato-flour, arrowroot, or *tous les mois*; pour boiling to them three-quarters of a pint more of milk, or of cream in preference: stir them well together, and then throw in two ounces of butter cut small. When this is melted, and well-beaten into the mixture, add the well-whisked yolks of four large or of five small eggs, half a teaspoonful of salt, something less of cayenne, and three ounces of lightly-grated cheese, Parmesan or English, or equal parts of both. Whisk the whites of the eggs to a quite firm and solid froth; then proceed, as for a *soufflé*, to mix and bake the *fondu*. Fill the *soufflé*-pan less than half full; set it instantly into the oven, which should be gentle, but not exceedingly slow, close the door immediately and do not open it for fifteen or twenty minutes: in from thirty to forty the *soufflé* will be ready for table unless the oven should be very cool: a fierce degree of heat will have a most unfavourable effect upon it.

## A COMMON OMLET

Six eggs are sufficient for an omlet of moderate size. Let them be very fresh; break them singly and carefully;

clear them from specks with the point of a fork while they are in the cup; or, when they are sufficiently whisked pour them through a sieve, and resume the beating until they are very light. Add to them from half to a whole teaspoonful of salt, and a seasoning of pepper. Dissolve in a small frying-pan a couple of ounces of butter, pour in the eggs, and as soon as the omlet is well risen and firm throughout, slide it on to a hot dish, fold it together like a turnover, and serve it *immediately*; from five to seven minutes will fry it.

Eggs, 6; butter, 2 oz; seasoning of salt and pepper: 5 to 7 minutes.

## PLAIN COMMON FRITTERS

Mix with three well-whisked eggs a quarter-pint of milk, and strain them through a fine sieve; add them gradually to three large tablespoonsful of flour, and thin the batter with as much more milk as will bring it to the consist-ence of cream; beat it up thoroughly at the moment of using it, that the fritters may be light. Drop it in small portions from a spouted jug or basin into boiling lard; when lightly coloured on one side, turn the fritters, drain them well from the lard as they are lifted out, and serve them very quickly. They are eaten generally with fine sugar, and orange or lemon juice: the first of these may be sifted quickly over them after they are dished, and the oranges or lemons halved or quartered, and sent to table with them. The lard used for frying them should be fresh and pure-flavoured: it renders them more crisp and light than butter, and is, therefore, better suited to the purpose. These fritters may be agreeably varied by mingling with the batter just before it is used two or three ounces of well cleaned and well dried currants, or three or four apples of a good boiling kind *not* very finely minced. Double the quantity of batter will be required for a large dish.

Eggs, 3; flour, 3 tablespoonsful; milk, ¼ to ½ pint.

# The Elegant Economist's Puddings

## GENERAL DIRECTIONS

Custard pudding to have a good appearance, must be *simmered* only but without ceasing; for if boiled in a quick and careless manner, the surface instead of being smooth and velvety, will be full of holes, or honey-combed, as it is called, and the whey will flow from it and mingle with the sauce. A thickly buttered sheet of writing-paper should be laid between the custard mixture and the cloth before it is tied over, or the cover of the mould is closed upon it; and the mould itself or the basin in which it is boiled, and which should always be quite full, must likewise be well buttered; and after it is lifted from the water the pudding should be left in it for quite five minutes before it is dished, to prevent its breaking or spreading about.

Batter is much lighter when boiled in a cloth, and allowed full room to swell, than when confined in a mould: it should be well beaten the instant before it is poured into it, and put into the water immediately after it is securely tied. The cloth should be moist and thickly floured, and the pudding should be sent to table as expeditiously as possible after it is done, as it will quickly become heavy. This applies equally to all puddings made with paste, which are rendered uneatable by any delay in serving them after they are ready: they should be opened a little at the top as soon as they are taken from the boiler or stewpan to permit the escape of the steam from within.

A *very* little salt improves all sweet puddings, by taking off the insipidity, and bringing out the full flavour of the other ingredients, but its presence should not be in the slightest degree *perceptible*. When brandy, wine, or lemon-juice is added to them it should be stirred in briskly, and by degrees, quite at last, as it would be likely otherwise to curdle the milk or eggs.


## TO MIX BATTER FOR PUDDINGS

Put the flour and salt into a bowl, and stir them together; whisk the eggs thoroughly, strain them through a fine hair-sieve, and add them *very gradually* to the flour; for if too much liquid be poured to it at once it will be full of lumps, and it is easy with care to keep the batter perfectly smooth. Beat it well and lightly with the back of a strong wooden spoon, and after the eggs are added thin it with milk to a proper consistence. The whites of the eggs beaten separately to a solid froth, and stirred gently into the mixture the instant before it is tied up for boiling, or before it is put into the oven to be baked, will render it remarkably light. When fruit is added to the batter, it must be made thicker than when it is served plain, or it will sink to the bottom of the pudding. Batter should never *stick to the knife* when it is sent to table: it will do this both when a sufficient number of eggs are not mixed with it, and when it is not enough cooked.

About four eggs to the half pound of flour will make it firm enough to cut smoothly.

## SUET CRUST, FOR MEAT OR FRUIT PUDDINGS

Clear off the skin from some fresh beef kidney-suet, hold it firmly with a fork, and with a sharp knife slice it thin, free it entirely from fibre, and mince it very fine: six ounces thus prepared will be found quite sufficient for a pound of flour. Mix them well together, add half a teaspoonful of salt for meat puddings, and a third as much for fruit ones, and sufficient cold water to make the whole into a very firm paste; work it smooth, and roll it out of equal thickness when it is used. The weight of suet should be taken after it is minced. This crust is so much lighter, and more wholesome than that which is made with butter, that we cannot refrain from recommending it in preference to our readers. Some cooks merely slice the suet in thin shavings, mix it with the flour, and beat the crust with a paste-roller, until the flour and suet are perfectly incorporated; but it is better minced.

Flour, 2 lb; suet, 12 oz; salt, 1 teaspoonful; water, 1 pint.

## BUTTER CRUST FOR PUDDINGS

When suet is disliked for crust, butter must supply its place, but there must be no intermixture of lard in paste which is to be boiled. Eight ounces to the pound of flour will render it sufficiently rich for most eaters, and less will generally be preferred; rich crust of this kind being more indigestible by far than that which is baked. The butter may be lightly broken into the flour before the water is added or it may be laid on, and rolled into the paste as for puff crust. A small portion of salt must be added to it always, and for a meat pudding the same proportion as directed in the preceding receipt. For kitchen, or for quite common family puddings, butter and clarified dripping are used sometimes in equal proportions. From three to four ounces of each will be sufficient for the pound and a quarter of flour.

Flour, 1 lb; butter, 8 oz; salt, for fruit puddings, ½ saltspoonful; for meat puddings, ½ teaspoonful.

## WINE SAUCE FOR SWEET PUDDINGS

Boil gently together for ten or fifteen minutes the very thin rind of half a small lemon, about an ounce and a half of sugar, and a wineglassful of water. Take out the lemon-peel and stir into the sauce until it has boiled for one minute, an ounce of butter smoothly mixed with a large half-teaspoonful of flour; add a wineglassful and a half of sherry or Madeira or other good white wine, and when quite hot serve the sauce without delay. Port wine sauce is made in the same way with the addition of a dessertspoonful of lemon-juice, some grated nutmeg and a little more sugar. Orange-rind and juice may be used for it instead of lemon.

## A GERMAN CUSTARD
## PUDDING-SAUCE

Boil very gently together half-pint of new milk or of milk and cream mixed, a very thin strip or two of fresh lemon-rind, a bit of cinnamon, half-inch of a vanilla bean, and an ounce and a half or two ounces of sugar, until the milk is strongly flavoured; then strain, and pour it, by slow degrees, to the well-beaten yolks of three eggs, smoothly mixed with a *knife-end-full* (about half a teaspoonful) of flour, a grain or two of salt, and a tablespoonful of cold milk; and stir these very quickly round as the milk is added. Put the sauce again into the stewpan, and whisk or stir it rapidly until it thickens, and looks creamy. It must not be placed *upon* the fire, but should be held over it, when this is done. The Germans *mill* their sauces to a froth; but they may be whisked with almost equally good effect, though a small mill for the purpose – formed like a chocolate mill – may be had at a very trifling cost.

## BATTER PUDDING

Mix the yolks of three eggs smoothly with three heaped tablespoonsful of flour, thin the batter with new milk until it is of the consistence of cream, whisk the whites of eggs apart, stir them into the batter, and boil the pudding in a floured cloth or in a buttered mould or basin for an hour. Before it is served, cut the top quickly into large dice half through the pudding, pour over it a small jarful of fine currant, raspberry, or strawberry jelly, and send it to table without the *slightest* delay.

Flour, 3 tablespoonsful; eggs, 3; salt, ½ teaspoonful; milk, from ½ to whole pint: 1 hour.

## HERODOTUS' PUDDING
### (*A Genuine Classical Receipt*)

'Prepare and mix in the usual manner one pound of fine raisins stoned, one pound of minced beef-suet, half a pound of bread-crumbs, four figs chopped small, two tablespoonsful of moist sugar (*honey*, in the original), two wineglassesful of sherry, and the rind of half a large lemon (grated). Boil the pudding for *fourteen hours*.'

*Obs.* This receipt is really to be found in Herodotus. The only variations made in it are the substitution of sugar for honey, and sherry for the wine of ancient Greece. We are indebted for it to an accomplished scholar, who has had it served at his own table on more than one occasion; and we have given it on his authority, without testing it: but we venture to suggest that *seven* hours would boil it quite sufficiently.

## THE PUBLISHER'S PUDDING

This pudding can scarcely be made *too* rich. First blanch, and then beat to the smoothest possible paste, six ounces of fresh Jordan almonds, and a dozen bitter ones; pour very gradually to them, in the mortar, three-quarters of a pint of boiling cream; then turn them into a cloth, and wring it from them again with strong expression. Heat a full half-pint of it afresh, and pour it, as soon as it boils, upon four ounces of fine bread-crumbs, set a plate over, and leave them to become nearly cold; then mix thoroughly with them four ounces of maccaroons, crushed tolerably small; five of finely minced beef-suet, five of marrow, cleared very carefully from fibre, and from the splinters of bone which are sometimes found in it, and shred not very small, two ounces of flour, six of pounded sugar, four of dried cherries, four of the best Muscatel raisins, weighed after they are stoned, half a pound of candied citron, or of citron and orange-rind mixed, a quarter saltspoonful of salt, half a nutmeg, the yolks only of seven full-sized eggs, the grated rind of a large lemon, and last of all, a glass of the best Cognac brandy, which must be stirred briskly in by slow degrees. Pour the mixture into a *thickly* buttered mould or basin, which contains a full quart, fill it to the brim, lay a sheet of buttered writing-paper over, then a well-floured cloth, tie them securely, and boil the pudding for four hours and a quarter; let it stand for two minutes before it is turned out; dish it carefully, and serve it with the German pudding-sauce of page 126.

Jordan almonds, 6 oz; bitter almonds, 12; cream, ¾ pint; bread-crumbs, 4 oz; cream wrung from almonds, ½ pint; crushed maccaroons, 4 oz; flour, 2 oz; beef-suet, 5 oz; marrow, 5 oz; dried cherries, 4 oz; stoned muscatel raisins, 4 oz; pounded sugar, 6 oz; candied citron (or citron and orange-rind mixed), ½ lb; pinch of salt; ½ nutmeg; grated rind, 1 lemon; yolks of eggs, 7; best cognac, 1 wineglassful: boiled in mould or basin, 4¼ hours.

*Obs.* This pudding, which, if well made, is very light

as well as rich, will be sufficiently good for most tastes without the almonds: when they are omitted, the boiling cream must be poured at once to the bread-crumbs.

## THE WELCOME GUEST'S OWN PUDDING
(*Light and Wholesome – Author's Receipt*)

Pour, quite boiling, on four ounces of fine bread-crumbs, an exact half-pint of new milk, or of thin cream; lay a plate over the basin and let them remain until cold; then stir to them four ounces of dry crumbs of bread, four of very finely minced beef kidney suet, a small pinch of salt, three ounces of coarsely crushed ratifias, three ounces of candied citron and orange-rind sliced thin, and the grated rind of one large or of two small lemons. Clear, and whisk four large eggs well, throw to them by degrees four ounces of pounded sugar, and continue to whisk them until it is dissolved, and they are very light; stir them to, and beat them well up with the other ingredients; pour the mixture into a thickly buttered mould, or basin which will contain nearly a quart, and which it should fill to within half-inch of the brim; lay first a buttered paper, then a well floured pudding-cloth over the top, tie them tightly and very securely round, gather up and fasten the corners of the cloth, and boil the pudding for two hours at the utmost. Let it stand for a minute or two before it is dished, and serve it with simple wine sauce; or with pine-apple or any other *clear* fruit-sauce.

Boil very gently, for about ten minutes, a full quarter-pint of water, with the very thin rind of half a fresh lemon, and an ounce and a half of lump sugar; then take out the lemon peel, and stir in a small teaspoonful of arrowroot, smoothly mixed with the strained juice of the lemon (with or without the addition of a little orange juice); take the sauce from the fire, throw in nearly half a glass of pale French brandy, or substitute for this a large wineglassful of sherry, or of any other white wine which may be preferred, but increase a little, in that case, the proportion of arrowroot.

## THE ELEGANT ECONOMIST'S PUDDING

Butter thickly a plain mould or basin, and line it entirely with slices of cold plum or raisin pudding, cut so as to join closely and neatly together; fill it quite with a good custard; lay, first a buttered paper, and then a floured cloth over it, tie them securely, and boil the pudding gently for an hour; let it stand for ten minutes after it is taken up before it is turned out of the mould. This is a more tasteful mode of serving the remains of a plum-pudding than the usual one of broiling them in slices, or converting them into fritters. The German sauce, well milled or frothed, is generally much relished with sweet boiled puddings, and adds greatly to their good appearance; but common wine or punch sauce, may be sent to table with the above quite as appropriately.

Mould or basin holding 1½ pint, lined with thin slices of plum-pudding; ¾ pint new milk boiled gently 5 minutes with grain of salt, 5 bitter almonds, bruised; sugar in lumps, 2½ oz; thin rind of ½ lemon, strained and mixed directly with 4 large well-beaten eggs; poured into mould while just warm: boiled gently 1 hour.

## SMALL AND VERY LIGHT PLUM PUDDING

With three ounces of the crumb of a stale loaf finely grated and soaked in a quarter-pint of boiling milk, mix six ounces of suet minced very small, one ounce of dry bread-crumbs, ten ounces of stoned raisins, a little salt, the grated rind of a China orange, and three eggs, leaving out one white. Boil the pudding for two hours, and serve it with very sweet sauce; put no sugar in it.

## THE AUTHOR'S CHRISTMAS PUDDING

To three ounces of flour, and the same weight of fine, lightly-grated bread-crumbs, add six of beef kidney-suet, chopped small, six of raisins, weighed after they are stoned, six of well-cleaned currants, four ounces of minced apples, five of sugar, two of candied orange-rind, half a teaspoonful of nutmeg, mixed with pounded mace, a very little salt, a small glass of brandy, and three whole eggs. Mix and beat these ingredients well together, tie them tightly in a thickly-floured cloth, and boil them for three hours and a half. We can recommend this as a remarkably light small rich pudding: it may be served with German wine, or punch sauce.

Flour, 3 oz; bread-crumbs, 3 oz; suet, stoned raisins, and currants, each, 6 oz; minced apples, 4 oz; sugar,

5 oz; candied peel, 2 oz; spice, ½ teaspoonful; salt, few grains; brandy, small wineglassful; eggs, 3: 3½ hours.

## SUFFOLK, OR HARD DUMPLINGS

Mix a little salt with some flour, and make it into smooth and rather lithe paste, with cold water or skimmed milk; form it into dumplings, and throw them into boiling water: in half an hour they will be ready to serve. A better kind of dumpling is made by adding sufficient milk to the flour to form a thick batter, and then tying the dumplings in small well-floured cloths. In Suffolk farmhouses, they are served with the dripping-pan gravy of roast meat; and they are sometimes made very small indeed, and boiled with stewed shin of beef.

## THE PRINTER'S PUDDING

Grate very lightly six ounces of the crumb of a stale loaf, and put it into a deep dish. Dissolve in a quart of cold new milk four ounces of good Lisbon sugar; add it to five large, well-whisked eggs, strain, and mix them with the bread-crumbs; stir in two ounces of a fresh finely-grated cocoa-nut; add a flavouring of nutmeg or of lemon-rind, and the slightest pinch of salt; let the pudding stand for a couple of hours to soak the bread; and bake it in a gentle oven for three-quarters of an hour: it will be excellent if carefully made, and not too quickly baked. When the cocoa-nut is not at hand, an ounce of butter just dissolved, should be poured over the dish before the crumbs are put into it; and the rind of an entire lemon may be used to give it flavour; but the cocoa-nut imparts a peculiar richness when it is good and fresh.

Bread-crumbs, 6 oz; new milk, 1 quart; sugar, 4 oz; eggs, 5; cocoa-nut, 2 oz (or rind, 1 large lemon, and 1 oz butter); slightest pinch of salt: to stand 2 hours. Baked in gentle oven full ¾ hour.

*Obs.* When a very sweet pudding is liked, the proportion of sugar may be increased.

## THE YOUNG WIFE'S PUDDING
### (*Author's Receipt*)

Break separately into a cup four perfectly sweet eggs, and with the point of a small three-pronged fork clear them from the specks. Throw them, as they are done, into a large basin, or a bowl, and beat them up lightly for four or five minutes; then add by degrees two ounces and a half of pounded sugar, with a very small pinch of salt, and whisk the mixture well, holding the fork rather loosely between the thumb and fingers; next, grate in the rind of a quite fresh lemon, or substitute for it a tablespoonful of lemon-brandy, or of orange-flower water, which should be thrown in by degrees and stirred briskly to the eggs. Add a pint of cold new milk, and pour the pudding into a well buttered dish. Slice some stale bread, something more than a quarter of an inch thick, and with a very small cake-cutter cut sufficient rounds from it to cover the top of the pudding; butter them thickly with good butter; lay them, with the dry side undermost, upon the pudding, sift sugar thickly on them, and set the dish gently into a Dutch or American oven, which should be placed at the distance of a foot or more from a moderate fire. An hour of very *slow baking* will be just sufficient to render the pudding firm throughout; but should the fire be fierce, or the oven placed too near it, the receipt will fail.

*Obs.* We give minute directions for this dish, because though simple, it is very delicate and good, and the same instructions will serve for all the varieties of it which follow. The cook who desires to succeed with them, must take the trouble to regulate properly the heat of the oven in which they are baked. When it is necessary to place them in that of the kitchen-range the door should be left open for a time to cool it down (should it be very hot), before they are placed in it; and they may be set upon a plate or dish reversed, if the iron should still remain greatly heated.

## THE GOOD DAUGHTER'S MINCEMEAT PUDDING
### (*Author's Receipt*)

Lay into a rather deep tart-dish some thin slices of French roll very slightly spread with butter and covered with a thick layer of mincemeat; place a second tier lightly on these, covered in the same way with the mincemeat; then pour gently in a custard made with three well-whisked eggs, three-quarters of a pint of new milk or thin cream, the slightest pinch of salt, and two ounces of sugar. Let the pudding stand to soak for an hour, then bake it gently until it is quite firm in the centre: this will be in from three-quarters of an hour to a full hour.

## BAKEWELL PUDDING

This pudding is famous not only in Derbyshire, but in several of our northern counties, where it is usually served on all holiday-occasions. Line a shallow tart-dish with quite an inch-deep layer of several kinds of good preserve mixed together, and intermingle with them from two to three ounces of candied citron or orange-rind. Beat well the yolks of ten eggs, and add to them gradually half a pound of sifted sugar; when they are well mixed, pour in by degrees half a pound of good clarified butter, and a little ratifia* or any other flavour that may be preferred; fill the dish two-thirds full with this mixture, and bake the pudding for nearly an hour in a moderate oven. Half the quantity will be sufficient for a small dish.

Mixed preserves, 1½ to 2 lb; yolks of eggs, 10; sugar, ½ lb; butter, ½ lb; ratifia, lemon-brandy, or other flavouring, to the taste: baked, moderate oven, ¾ to 1 hour.

*Obs.* This is a rich and expensive, but not very refined pudding. A variation of it, known in the south as an Alderman's Pudding, is we think, superior to it. It is made without the candied peel, and with a layer of apricot-jam only, six ounces of butter, six of sugar, the yolks of six, and the whites of two eggs.

* [*A liqueur flavoured with almonds or peach kernels.*]

# THE ELEGANT ECONOMIST'S PUDDING

We have already given a receipt for an exceedingly good boiled pudding bearing this title, but we think the baked one answers even better, and it is made with rather more facility. Butter a deep tart-dish well, cut the slices of plum-pudding to join exactly in lining it, and press them against it lightly to make them adhere, as without this precaution they are apt to float off; pour in as much custard (previously thickened and left to become cold), or any other sweet pudding mixture, as will fill the dish almost to the brim; cover the top with thin slices of the plum pudding, and bake it in a slow oven from thirty minutes to a full hour, according to the quantity and quality of the contents. One pint of new milk poured boiling on an ounce and a half of *tous-les-mois*, smoothly mixed with a quarter of a pint of cold milk, makes with the addition of four ounces of sugar, four small eggs, a little lemon-grate, and two or three bitter almonds, or a few drops of ratifia, an excellent pudding of this kind; it should be baked nearly three-quarters of an hour in quite a slow oven. Two ounces and a half of arrowroot may be used in lieu of the *tous-les-mois*.

## SUTHERLAND, OR CASTLE PUDDINGS

Take an equal weight of eggs in the shell, of good butter, of fine dry flour, and of sifted sugar. First, whisk the eggs for ten minutes or until they appear extremely light: then throw in the sugar by degrees, and continue the whisking for four or five minutes; next, strew in the flour, also gradually, and when it appears smoothly blended with the other ingredients, pour the butter to them in small portions, each of which should be beaten in until there is no appearance of it left. It should previously be just liquefied with the least possible degree of heat: this may be effected by putting it into a well-warmed saucepan, and shaking it round until it is dissolved. A grain or two of salt should be thrown in with the flour; and the rind of half a fine lemon rasped on sugar or grated, or some pounded mace, or any other flavour can be added at choice. Pour the mixture directly it is ready into well-buttered cups, and bake the puddings from twenty to twenty-five minutes. When cold they resemble good pound cakes, and may be served as such. Wine sauce should be sent to table with them.

Eggs, 4; their weight in flour, sugar, and butter; *little* salt; flavouring of pounded mace or lemon-rind.

*Obs.* Three eggs are sufficient for a small dish of these puddings, They may be varied with an ounce or two of candied citron; or with a spoonful of brandy, or a little orange-flower water. The mode we have given of making them will be found perfectly successful if our directions be followed with exactness. In a slow oven they will not be too much baked in half an hour.


## POTATO PUDDING

With a pound and a quarter of fine mealy potatoes, boiled very dry, and mashed perfectly smooth while hot, mix three ounces of butter, five or six of sugar, five eggs, a few grains of salt, and the grated rind of a small lemon. Pour the mixture into a well-buttered dish, and bake it in a moderate oven for nearly three-quarters of an hour. It should be turned out and sent to table with fine sugar sifted over it, or for variety, red currant jelly, or any other preserve, may be spread on it as soon as it is dished.

Potatoes, 1¼ lb; butter, 3 oz; sugar, 5 or 6 oz; eggs, 5 or 6; lemon-rind, 1; salt, few grains: 40 to 45 minutes.

*Obs.* When cold, this pudding eats like cake, and may be served as such, omitting of course, the sugar or preserve when it is dished.

## THE POOR AUTHOR'S PUDDING

Flavour a quart of new milk by boiling in it for a few minutes half a stick of well-bruised cinnamon, or the thin rind of a small lemon; add a few grains of salt, and three ounces of sugar, and turn the whole into a deep basin: when it is quite cold, stir to it three well-beaten eggs, and strain the mixture into a pie-dish. Cover the top entirely with slices of bread free from crust, and half an inch thick, cut so as to join neatly, and buttered on both sides: bake the pudding in a moderate oven for about half an hour, or in a Dutch oven before the fire.

New milk, 1 quart; cinnamon, or lemon-rind; sugar, 3 oz; little salt; eggs, 3; buttered bread: baked ½ hour.

## THE CURATE'S PUDDING

Wash, wipe, and pare some quickly grown rhubarb-stalks, cut them into short lengths, and put a layer of them into a deep dish with a spoonful or two of Lisbon sugar; cover these evenly with part of a penny roll [*or thin slices of bread*] sliced thin; and add another thick layer of fruit and sugar, then one of bread, then another of the rhubarb; cover this last with a deep layer of fine bread-crumbs well mingled with about a tablespoonful of sugar, pour a little clarified butter over them, and send the pudding to a brisk oven. From thirty to forty minutes will bake it. Good boiling apples sliced, sweetened, and flavoured with nutmeg or grated lemon-rind, and covered with well buttered slices of bread, make an excellent pudding of this kind, and so do black currants likewise, without the butter.

# Sweet Poisons and
# Superlative Preserves

## GENERAL REMARKS ON CAKES

We have inserted here but a comparatively limited number of receipts for these 'sweet poisons', as they have been emphatically called, and we would willingly have diminished still further even the space which has been allotted to them, that we might have had room in their stead for others of a more really useful character; but we have felt reluctant to withdraw such a portion of any of the chapters as might materially alter the original character of the work, or cause dissatisfaction to any of our kind readers; we will therefore content ourselves with remarking, that more illness is caused by habitual indulgence in the richer and heavier kinds of cakes than could easily be credited by persons who have given no attention to the subject.

Amongst those which have the worst effects are almond, and plum *pound* cakes, as they are called; all varieties of the *brioche* and such others as contain a large quantity of butter and eggs.

The least objectionable are simple buns, biscuits, yeast and sponge cakes, and *meringues*; these last being extremely light and delicate, and made of white of egg and sugar only, are really not unwholesome.

## TO PREPARE BUTTER
## FOR RICH CAKES

For all large and very rich cakes the usual directions are, *to heat the butter to a cream*; but we find that they are quite as light when it is cut small and gently melted with just so much heat as will dissolve it, and no more. If it be shaken round in a saucepan previously warmed, and held near the fire for a short time, it will soon be liquefied, which is all that is required: it must on no account be *hot* when it is added to the other ingredients, to which it must be poured in small portions after they are all mixed, in the way which we have minutely described in the receipt for a Madeira cake [p. 127], and that of the Sutherland puddings [p. 120]. To *cream* it, drain the water well from it after it is cut, soften it a little before the fire should it be very hard, and then with the back of a large strong wooden spoon beat it until it resembles thick cream. When prepared thus, the sugar is added to it first, and then the other ingredients in succession. For plum cakes it is better creamed than liquefied, as the fruit requires a paste of some consistence to prevent its sinking to the bottom of the mould in which it is baked. For plain seed-cakes the more simple plan answers perfectly.

## ALMOND MACAROONS

Blanch a pound of fresh Jordan almonds, wipe them dry, and set them into a very cool oven to render them perfectly so; pound them to an exceedingly smooth paste, with a little white of egg, then whisk to a firm solid froth the white of seven eggs, or of eight, should they be small; mix with them a pound and a half of the finest sugar; add these by degrees to the almonds, whisk the whole up well together, and drop the mixture upon wafer-paper, which may be procured at the confectioner's: bake the cakes in a moderate oven a very pale brown. It is an improvement to their flavour to substitute an ounce of bitter almonds for one of the sweet. They are sometimes made with an equal weight of each; and another variety of them is obtained by gently browning the almonds in a slow oven before they are pounded.

Jordan almonds blanched, 1 lb; sugar, 1½ lb; whites of 7 or 8 eggs: 15 to 20 minutes.

## IMPERIALS
### (*Not very rich*)

Work into a pound of flour six ounces of butter, and mix well with them half a pound of sifted sugar, six ounces of currants, two ounces of candied orange-peel, the grated rind of a lemon, and four well-beaten eggs. Flour a tin lightly, and with a couple of forks place the paste upon it in small rough heaps quite two inches apart. Bake them in a very gentle oven, from a quarter of an hour to twenty minutes, or until they are equally coloured to a pale brown.

Flour, 1 lb; butter, 6 oz; sugar, 8 oz; currants, 6 oz; candied peel, 2 oz; rind of 1 lemon; eggs, 4: 15 to 20 minutes.

## PLAIN POUND OR
## CURRANT CAKE
### (*Or rich Brawn Brack, or Borrow Brack*)

Mix ten eggs (some cooks take a pound in weight of these), one pound of sugar, one of flour, and as much of butter. For a plum cake, let the butter be worked to a cream; add the sugar to it first, then the yolks of the eggs, next stir lightly in the whites, after which, add one pound of currants and the candied peel, and, last of all, the flour by degrees, and a glass of brandy when it is liked. Nearly or quite two hours' baking will be required for this, and one hour for half the quantity.

To convert the above into the popular Irish 'speckled bread', or *Brawn Brack* of the richer kind, add to it three ounces of carraway-seeds: these are sometimes used in combination with the currants, but more commonly without.

## A GOOD MADEIRA CAKE

Whisk four fresh eggs until they are as light as possible, then, continuing still to whisk them, throw in by *slow* degrees the following ingredients in the order in which they are written: six ounces of dry, pounded, and sifted sugar; six of flour, also dried and sifted; four ounces of butter just dissolved, but not heated; the rind of a fresh lemon; and the instant before the cake is moulded, beat well in the third of a teaspoonful of carbonate of soda: bake it an hour in a moderate oven. In this, as in all compositions of the same nature, observe particularly that each portion of butter must be beaten into the mixture until no appearance of it remains before the next is added; and if this be done, and the preparation be kept light by constant and light whisking, the cake will be as good, if not better, than if the butter were creamed. Candied citron can be added to the paste, but it is not needed.

Eggs, 4; sugar, 6 oz; flour, 6 oz; butter, 4 oz; rind of 1 lemon; carbonate of soda, ⅓ of teaspoonful: 1 hour, moderate oven.

## ACTON GINGERBREAD

Whisk four strained or well-cleared eggs to the lightest possible froth and pour to them, by degrees, a pound and a quarter of treacle, still beating them lightly. Add, in the same manner, six ounces of pale brown sugar free from lumps, one pound of sifted flour, and six ounces of good butter, *just* sufficiently warmed to be liquid, and no more, for if hot, it would render the cake heavy; it should be poured in small portions to the mixture, which should be well beaten up with the back of a wooden spoon as each portion is thrown in: the success of the cake depends almost entirely on this part of the process. When properly mingled with the mass, the butter will not be perceptible on the surface; and if the cake be kept light by constant whisking; large bubbles will appear in it to the last. When it is so far ready, add to it one ounce of Jamaica ginger and a large teaspoonful of cloves in fine powder, with the lightly grated rinds of two fresh full-sized lemons. Butter thickly, in every part, a shallow square tin pan, and bake the gingerbread slowly for nearly or quite an hour in a gentle oven. Let it cool a little before it is turned out, and set it on its edge until cold, supporting it, if needful, against a large jar or bowl. We have usually had it baked in an American oven, in a tin less than two inches deep; and it has been excellent. We retain the name given to it originally in our own circle.

## QUEEN CAKES*

To make these, proceed exactly as for the pound currant cake of page 127, but bake the mixture in small well-buttered tin pans (heart-shaped ones are usual), in a somewhat brisk oven, for about twenty minutes.

## JUMBLES

Rasp in some good sugar the rinds of two lemons; dry, reduce it to powder, and sift it with as much more as will make up a pound in weight; mix with it one pound of flour, four well-beaten eggs, and six ounces of warm butter: drop the mixture on buttered tins, and bake the jumbles in a *very* slow oven from twenty to thirty minutes. They should be pale, but perfectly crisp.

---

* [*These, in some books are called simply 'Heart Cakes' and were, with cider, a speciality of some of the inns near London in the eighteenth century.*]

## THREADNEEDLE STREET BISCUITS

Mix with two pounds of sifted flour of the very best quality three ounces of good butter, and work it into the smallest possible crumbs; add four ounces of fine, dry, sifted sugar, and make them into a firm paste with new milk; beat this forcibly for some time with a rolling-pin, and when it is extremely smooth roll it the third of an inch thick, cut it with a small square cutter, and bake the biscuits in a very slow oven until they are crisp to the centre: no part of them should remain soft. Half a teaspoonful of carbonate of soda is said to improve them, but we have not put it to the test. Carraway-seeds can be added when they are liked.

Flour, 2 lb; butter, 3 oz; sugar, 4 oz; new milk, 1 pint or more: biscuits *slowly* baked until crisp.

## AUNT CHARLOTTE'S BISCUITS

These biscuits, which are very simple and very good, may be made with the same dough as fine white bread, with the addition of from half to a whole ounce of butter to the pound kneaded into it after it has risen. Break the butter small, spread out the dough a little, knead it in well and equally, and leave it for about half an hour to rise; then roll it a quarter of an inch thick, prick it well all over, cut out the biscuits, and bake them in a moderate oven from ten to fifteen minutes: they should be crisp quite through, but not deeply coloured.

White-bread dough, 2 lb; butter, 1 to 2 oz; to rise ½ hour. Baked in moderate oven 10 to 15 minutes.

## PREPARED, APPLE OR QUINCE JUICE

Pour into a clean earthen pan two quarts of spring water, and throw into it as quickly as they can be pared, quartered, and weighed, four pounds of nonsuches, pearmains, Ripstone pippins, or any other good boiling apples of fine flavour. When all are done, stew them gently until they are well broken, but not reduced quite to pulp; turn them into a jelly-bag, or strain the juice from them without pressure through a closely-woven cloth, which should be gathered over the fruit, and tied, and suspended above a deep pan until the juice ceases to drop from it: this, if not very clear, must be rendered so before it is used for syrup or jelly, but for all other purposes once straining it will be sufficient. Quinces are prepared in the same way, and with the same propor- tions of fruit and water, but they must not be too long boiled, or the juice will become red. We have found it answer well to have them simmered until they are per- fectly tender, and then to leave them with their liquor in a bowl until the following day, when the juice will be rich and clear. They should be thrown into the water very quickly after they are pared and weighed, as the air will soon discolour them. The juice will form a jelly much more easily if the cores and pips be left in the fruit.

Water, 2 quarts; apples or quinces, 4 lb.

## ORANGES FILLED WITH JELLY

This is one of the fanciful dishes which make a pretty appearance on a supper table, and are acceptable when much variety is desired. Take some very fine China oranges, and with the point of a small knife cut out from the top of each a round about the size of a shilling; then with the small end of a tea or an egg spoon, empty them entirely, taking great care not to break the rinds. Throw these into cold water, and make jelly of the juice, which must be well pressed from the pulp, and strained as clear as possible. Colour one half a fine rose colour with prepared cochineal, and leave the other very pale; when it is nearly cold, drain and wipe the orange-rinds, and fill them with alternate stripes of the two jellies; when they are perfectly cold cut them into quarters, and dispose them tastefully in a dish with a few light branches of myrtle between them. Calf's feet or any other variety of jelly, or different blanc-manges, may be used at choice to fill the rinds; the colours, however, should contrast as much as possible.

## QUEEN MAB'S PUDDING
*(An Elegant Summer Dish)*

Throw into a pint of new milk the thin rind of a small lemon, and six or eight bitter almonds, blanched and bruised; or substitute for these half a pod of vanilla cut small, heat it slowly by the side of the fire, and keep it at the point of boiling until it is strongly flavoured, then add a small pinch of salt, and three-quarters of an ounce of the finest isinglass, or a full ounce should the weather be extremely warm; when this is dissolved, strain the milk through a muslin, and put it into a clean saucepan, with from four to five ounces and a half of sugar in lumps, and half-pint of rich cream; give the whole one boil, and then stir it, briskly and by degrees, to the well-beaten yolks of six fresh eggs; next, thicken the mixture as a custard, over a gentle fire, but do not hazard its curdling; when it is of tolerable consistence, pour it out, and continue the stirring until it is half cold, then mix with it an ounce and a half of candied citron, cut in small spikes, and a couple of ounces of dried cherries, and pour it into a mould rubbed with a drop of oil: when turned out it will have the appearance of a pudding. From two to three ounces of preserved ginger, well drained and sliced, may be substituted for the cherries, and an ounce of pistachio-nuts, blanched and split, for the citron; these will make an elegant variety of the dish, and the syrup of the ginger, poured round as sauce, will be a further improvement. Currants steamed until tender, and candied orange or lemon-rind, are often used instead of the cherries, and the well-sweetened juice of strawberries, raspberries (white or red), apricots, peaches, or syrup of pine-apple, will make an agreeable sauce; a small quantity of this last will also give a delicious flavour to the pudding itself, when mixed with the other ingredients. Cream may be substituted entirely for the milk, when its richness is considered desirable.

New milk, 1 pint; rind 1 small lemon; bitter almonds,

6 to 8 (or, vanilla, ½ pod); salt, few grains; isinglass, ¾ oz (1 oz in sultry weather); sugar, 4½ oz; cream, ½ pint; yolks, 6 eggs; dried cherries, 2 oz; candied citron, 1½ oz; (or, preserved ginger, 2 to 3 oz and the syrup as sauce, and 1 oz of blanched pistachio-nuts; or 4 oz currants steamed 20 minutes, and 2 oz candied orange-rind). For sauce, sweetened juice of strawberries, raspberries, or plums, or pine-apple syrup.

*Obs.* The currants should be steamed in an earthen cullender, placed over a saucepan of boiling water, and covered with the lid. It will be a *great* improvement to place the pudding over ice for an hour before it is served.

## VERY GOOD LEMON CREAMS MADE WITHOUT CREAM

Pour over the very thin rinds of two moderate-sized but perfectly sound fresh lemons and six ounces of sugar, half-pint of spring water, and let them remain for six hours; then add the strained juice of the lemons, and five fresh eggs well beaten and also strained; take out the lemon-rind, and stir the mixture without ceasing over a gentle fire until it has boiled softly from six to eight minutes: it will not curdle as it would did milk supply the place of the water and lemon-juice. The creams are, we think, more delicate, though not quite so thick, when the yolks only of six eggs are used for them. They will keep well for nearly a week in really cold weather.

Rinds of lemons, 2; sugar, 6 oz (or 8 when a very sweet

dish is preferred); cold water, ½ pint: 6 hours. Juice of lemons, 2; eggs, 5: to be boiled softly 6 to 8 minutes.

*Obs.* Lemon creams may, on occasion, be more expeditiously prepared, by rasping the rind of the fruit upon the sugar which is used for them; or, by paring it thin, and boiling it for a few minutes with the lemon-juice, sugar, and water, before they are stirred to the eggs.

## RICH BOILED CUSTARD

Take a small cupful from a quart of fresh cream, and simmer the remainder for a few minutes with four ounces of sugar and the rind of a lemon, or give it any other flavour that may be preferred. Beat and strain the yolks of eight eggs, mix them with the cupful of cream, and stir the rest boiling to them: thicken the custard in a deep jug set over the fire in a pan of boiling water.

Cream, 1 quart; sugar, 4 oz; yolks of eggs, 8.

## THE QUEEN'S CUSTARD

On the beaten and strained yolks of twelve new-laid eggs pour a pint and a half of boiling cream which has been sweetened, with three ounces of sugar; add the smallest pinch of salt, and thicken the custard as usual. When nearly cold, flavour it with a glass and a half of noyau, maraschino, or cuirasseau [*curaçao*], and add the sliced almonds or not, at pleasure.

Yolks of eggs, 12; cream, 1½ pint; sugar, 3 oz; little salt; noyau, maraschino, or cuirasseau, 1½ wineglassful.

## CHOCOLATE CUSTARDS

Dissolve gently by the side of the fire an ounce and a half of the best chocolate in rather more than a wineglassful of water, and then boil it until it is perfectly smooth; mix with it a pint of milk well flavoured with lemon peel or vanilla, add two ounces of fine sugar, and when the whole boils, stir it to five well-beaten eggs which have been strained. Put the custard into a jar or jug, set it into a pan of boiling water, and stir it without ceasing until it is thick. Do not put it into glasses or a dish until it is nearly or quite cold. These, as well as all other custards, are infinitely finer when made with the yolks only of the eggs, of which the number must then be increased. Two ounces of chocolate, a pint of milk, half-pint of cream, two or three ounces of sugar, and eight yolks of eggs, will make very superior custards of this kind.

Rasped chocolate, 1½ oz; water, 1 *large* wineglassful: 5 to 8 minutes. New milk, 1 pint; eggs, 5; sugar, 2 oz. Or: chocolate, 2 oz; water, ¼ pint; new milk, 1 pint; sugar, 2½ to 3 oz; cream, ½ pint; yolks of eggs, 8.

*Obs.* Either of these may be moulded by dissolving from half to three-quarters of an ounce of isinglass in the milk. The proportion of chocolate can be increased to the taste.

## QUINCE OR APPLE CUSTARDS

Add to a pint of apple-juice prepared as for jelly, a table-spoonful of strained lemon-juice, and from four to six ounces of sugar according to the acidity of the fruit; stir these boiling, quickly, and in small portions, to eight well-beaten eggs, and thicken the custard in a jug placed in a pan of boiling water, in the usual manner. A large proportion of lemon-juice and a high flavouring of a rind can be given when approved. For quince custards, which if well made are excellent, observe the same directions as for the apple, but omit the lemon-juice. As we have before observed, all custards are much finer when made with the yolks only of the eggs, of which the number must be increased nearly half, when this is done.

Prepared apple-juice (see page 131), 1 pint; lemon-juice, 1 tablespoonful; sugar, 4 to 6 oz; eggs, 8. Quince custards, same proportions, but no lemon-juice.

*Obs.* In making lemon creams, the apple-juice may be substituted very advantageously for water, without varying the receipt in other respects.

## AN APPLE CHARLOTTE, OR CHARLOTTE DE POMMES

Butter a plain mould (a round or square cake-tin will answer the purpose quite well), and line it entirely with thin slices of the crumb of a stale loaf [*i.e. slices of bread with the crusts removed*], cut so as to fit into it with great exactness, and dipped into clarified butter. When this is done, fill the mould to the brim with apple marmalade; cover the top with slices of bread dipped in butter, and on these place a dish, a large plate, or the cover of a French stewpan with a weight upon it. Send the Charlotte to a brisk oven for three-quarters of an hour should it be small, and for an hour if large. Turn it out with great care, and serve it hot. If baked in a slack oven it will not take a proper degree of colour, and it will be liable to break in the dishing. The strips of bread must of course join very perfectly for if any spaces were left between them the syrup of the fruit would escape and destroy the good appearance of the dish: should there not have been sufficient marmalade prepared to fill the mould entirely, a jar of quince or apricot jam, or of preserved cherries even, may be added to it with advantage. The butter should be well drained from the Charlotte before it is taken from the mould; and sugar may be sifted thickly over it before it is served, or it may be covered with any kind of clear red jelly.

A more elegant, and we think an easier mode of forming the crust, is to line the mould with small rounds of bread stamped out with a plain cake or paste cutter, then dipped in butter, and placed with the edges sufficiently one over the other to hold the fruit securely: the strips of bread are sometimes arranged in the same way.

¾ to 1 hour, quick oven.


## BERMUDA WITCHES

Slice equally some rice, pound, or Savoy cake, not more than the sixth of an inch thick; take off the brown edges, and spread one half of it with Guava jelly, or, if more convenient, with fine strawberry, raspberry, or currant jelly of the best quality; on this strew thickly some fresh cocoa-nut grated small and lightly; press over it the remainder of the cake, and trim the whole into good form; divide the slices if large, pile them slopingly in the centre of a dish upon a very white napkin folded flat, and garnish or intersperse them with small sprigs of myrtle. For very young people a French roll or two, and good currant jelly, red or white, will supply a wholesome and inexpensive dish.

## A FEW GENERAL RULES AND DIRECTIONS FOR PRESERVING

1. Let everything used for the purpose be delicately clean and *dry*; bottles especially so.

2. Never place a preserving pan *flat upon the fire*, as this will render the preserve liable to *burn to*, as it is called; that is to say, to adhere closely to the metal, and then to burn; it should rest always on a trivet, or on the lowered bar of a kitchen range when there is no regular preserving stove in a house.

3. After the sugar is added to them, stir the preserves gently at first, and more quickly towards the end, without quitting them until they are done: this precaution will always prevent the chance of their being spoiled.

4. All preserves should be perfectly cleared from the scum as it rises.

5. Fruit which is to be preserved in syrup must first be blanched or boiled gently, until it is sufficiently softened to absorb the sugar; and a thin syrup must be poured on it at first, or it will shrivel instead of remaining plump, and becoming clear. Thus, if its weight of

sugar is to be allowed, and boiled to a syrup with a pint of water to the pound, only half the weight must be taken at first, and this must not be boiled with the water more than fifteen or twenty minutes at the commencement of the process; a part of the remaining sugar must be added every time the syrup is re-boiled, unless it should be otherwise directed in the receipt.

6. To preserve both the true flavour and the colour of fruit in jams and jellies, boil them rapidly until they are well reduced, *before* the sugar is added, and quickly afterwards, but do not allow them to become so much thickened that the sugar will not dissolve in them easily, and throw up its scum. In some seasons, the juice is so much richer than in others, that this effect takes place almost before one is aware of it; but the drop which adheres to the skimmer when it is held up, will show the state it has reached.

7. Never use tin, iron, or pewter spoons, or skimmers, for preserves, as they will convert the colour of red fruit into a dingy purple, and impart, besides, a very unpleasant flavour.*

8. When cheap jams or jellies are required, make them at once with Lisbon sugar, but use that which is *well refined* always, for preserves in general; it is a false economy, as we have elsewhere observed, to purchase an inferior kind, as there is great waste from it in the quantity of scum which it throws up. The *best* has been used for all the receipts given here.

9. Let fruit for preserving be gathered always in perfectly

* [*Use a wooden spoon only.*]

dry weather, and be free both from the morning and evening dew, and as much so as possible from dust. When bottled, it must be steamed or baked during the day on which it is gathered, or there will be a great loss from the bursting of the bottles; and for jams and jellies it cannot be too soon boiled down after it is taken from the trees.

## GREEN GOOSEBERRY JELLY

Wash some freshly gathered gooseberries very clean; after having taken off the tops and stalks, then to each pound pour three-quarters of a pint of spring water, and simmer them until they are well broken; turn the whole into a jelly-bag or cloth, and let all the juice drain through; weigh and boil it rapidly for fifteen minutes. Draw it from the fire, and stir in it until entirely dissolved, an equal weight of good sugar reduced to powder; boil the jelly from fifteen to twenty minutes longer, or until it jellies strongly on the spoon or skimmer; clear it perfectly from scum, and pour it into small jars, moulds, or glasses. It ought to be very pale and transparent. The sugar may be added to the juice at first, and the preserve boiled from twenty-five to thirty-five minutes, but the colour will not then be so good. When the fruit abounds, the juice may be drawn from it with very little water, when it will require much less boiling.

Gooseberries, 6 lb; water, 4½ pints: 20 to 30 minutes. Juice boiled quickly, 15 minutes; to each pound, 1 lb sugar: 15 to 20 minutes.

## STRAWBERRY JAM

Strip the stalks from some fine scarlet strawberries, weigh, and boil them for thirty-five minutes, keeping them very constantly stirred: throw in eight ounces of good sugar, beaten small, to the pound of fruit; mix them well off the fire, then boil the preserve again quickly for twenty-five minutes.

Strawberries, 6 lb: 35 minutes. Sugar, 3 lb: 25 minutes.

*Obs.* We do not think it needful to give directions with each separate receipt for skimming the preserve with care, and keeping it constantly stirred, but neither should in any case be neglected.

## TO PRESERVE STRAWBERRIES OR RASPBERRIES, FOR CREAMS OR ICES, WITHOUT BOILING

Let the fruit be gathered in the middle of a warm day, in very dry weather; strip it from the stalks directly, weigh it, bruise it *slightly*, turn it into a bowl or deep pan, and mix with it an equal weight of fine dry sifted sugar, and put it immediately into small, wide-necked bottles; cork these firmly without delay, and tie bladders over the tops. Keep them in a cool place, or the fruit will ferment. The mixture should be stirred softly, and only just suffi-ciently to blend the sugar and the fruit. The bottles must be perfectly dry, and the bladders, after having been cleaned in the usual way, and allowed to become nearly so, should be moistened with a little spirit on the side which is to be next to the cork. Unless these precautions be observed, there will be some danger of the whole being spoiled.

Equal weight of fruit and sugar.

## SUPERLATIVE RED CURRANT JELLY
### (*Norman Receipt*)

Strip carefully from the stems some quite ripe currants of the finest quality, and mix with them an equal weight of good sugar reduced to powder; boil these together quickly for exactly eight minutes, keep them stirred all the time, and clear off the scum – which will be very abundant – as it rises; then turn the preserve into a very clean sieve, and put into small jars the jelly which runs through it, and which will be delicious in flavour, and of the brightest colour. It should be carried immediately, when this is practicable, to an extremely cool but not a damp place, and left there until perfectly cold. The currants which remain in the sieve make an excellent jam, particularly if only part of the jelly be taken from them. In Normandy, where the fruit is of richer quality than in England, this preserve is boiled only two minutes, and is both firm and beautifully transparent.

Currants, 3 lb; sugar, 3 lb: 8 minutes.

*Obs.* This receipt we are told by some of our correspondents is not generally quite successful in this country, as the jelly, though it keeps well and is of the finest possible flavour, is scarcely firm enough for table. We have ourselves found this to be the case in cold damp seasons; but the preserve even then was valuable for many purposes, and always agreeable eating.

## BLACK CURRANT JAM
## AND MARMALADE

No fruit jellies so easily as black currants when they are ripe; and their juice is so rich and thick that it will bear the addition of a very small quantity of water sometimes, without causing the preserve to mould.

To six pounds of the fruit, stripped carefully from the stalks, add four pounds and a half of sugar. Let them heat gently, but as soon as the sugar is dissolved boil the preserve rapidly for fifteen minutes. A more common kind of jam may be made by boiling the fruit by itself from ten to fifteen minutes, and for ten minutes after half its weight of sugar has been added to it.

Black currants, 6 lb; sugar, 4½ lb: 15 minutes. Or: fruit, 6 lb: 10 to 15 minutes. Sugar, 3 lb: 10 minutes.

*Obs.* There are few preparations of fruit so refreshing and so useful in illness as those of black currants, and it is therefore advisable always to have a store of them, and to have them well and carefully made.

## NURSERY PRESERVE

Take the stones from a couple of pounds of Kentish cherries, and boil them twenty minutes; then add to them a pound and a half of raspberries, and an equal quantity of red and of white currants, all weighed after they have been cleared from their stems. Boil these together quickly for twenty minutes; mix with them three pounds and a quarter of common sugar, and give the preserve fifteen minutes more of quick boiling. A pound and a half of gooseberries may be substituted for the cherries; but they will not require any stewing before they are added to the other fruits. The jam must be well stirred from the beginning, or it will burn to the pan.

Kentish cherries, 2 lb: 20 minutes. Raspberries, red currants, and white currants, of each 1½ lb: 20 minutes. Sugar, 3¼ lb: 15 minutes.


## DAMSON JAM
### (*Very good*)

The fruit for this jam should be freshly gathered and quite ripe. Split, stone, weigh, and boil it quickly for forty minutes; then stir in half its weight of good sugar roughly powdered, and when it is dissolved, give the preserve fifteen minutes additional boiling, keeping it stirred, and thoroughly skimmed.

Damsons, stoned, 6 lb: 40 minutes. Sugar, 3 lb: 15 minutes.

*Obs.* A more refined preserve is made by pressing the fruit through a sieve after it is boiled tender; but the jam is excellent without.


## QUINCE JELLY

Pare, quarter, core, and weigh some ripe but quite sound quinces, as quickly as possible, and throw them as they are done into part of the water in which they are to be boiled, as directed at page 131, allow one pint of this to each pound of the fruit, and simmer it gently until it is a little broken, but not so long as to redden the juice, which ought to be very pale. Turn the whole into a jelly-bag, or strain the liquid through a fine cloth, and let it drain very closely from it but without the slightest pressure. Weigh the juice, put it into a delicately clean preserving pan, and boil it quickly for twenty minutes; take it from the fire and stir in it, until it is entirely dissolved, twelve ounces of sugar for each pound of juice, or fourteen ounces if the fruit should be very acid, which it will be in the earlier part of the season; keep it constantly stirred and throughly cleared from scum, from ten to twenty minutes longer, or until it jellies strongly in falling from the skimmer; then pour it directly into glasses or moulds. If properly made, it will be sufficiently firm to turn out of the latter, and it will be beautifully transparent, and rich in flavour. It may be made with an equal weight of juice and sugar mixed together in the first instance, and boiled from twenty to thirty minutes. It is difficult to state the time precisely, because from different causes it will vary much. It should be reduced rapidly to the proper point, as long boiling injures the colour: this is always more perfectly preserved by boiling the juice without the sugar first.

To each pound pared and cored quinces, 1 pint water: ¾ to 1½ hour. Juice, boiled 20 minutes. To each pound, 12 oz sugar: 10 to 20 minutes. Or, juice and sugar equal weight: 20 to 30 minutes.

This is delicious used instead of red currant jelly with meat.

## QUINCE MARMALADE

When to economize the fruit is not an object, pare, core, and quarter some of the inferior quinces, and boil them in as much water as will nearly cover them, until they begin to break; strain the juice from them and for the marmalade put half a pint of it to each pound of fresh quinces: in preparing these, be careful to cut out the hard stone parts round the cores. Simmer them gently until they are perfectly tender, then press them, with the juice, through a coarse sieve; put them into a perfectly clean pan, and boil them until they form almost a dry paste; add for each pound of quinces and the half-pint of juice, three-quarters of a pound of sugar in fine powder, and boil the marmalade for half an hour, stirring it gently without ceasing: it will be very firm and bright in colour. If made shortly after the fruit is gathered, a little additional sugar will be required; and when a richer and less dry marmalade is better liked, it must be boiled for a shorter time, and an equal weight of fruit and sugar may be used.

Quinces, pared and cored, 4 lb; prepared juice, 1 quart: 2 to 3 hours. Boiled fast to dry, 20 to 40 minutes. Sugar, 3 lb: 30 minutes.

Richer marmalade: quinces, 4 lb; juice, 1 quart; sugar, 4 lb.

# The Counsellor's Cup: Syrups and Liqueurs

## FINE CURRANT SYRUP, OR SIROP DE GROSEILLES

Express the juice from some fine ripe red currants, which have been gathered in dry weather, and stripped from the stalks; strain, and put it into a new, or a perfectly clean and dry earthen pitcher, and let it stand in a cellar or in some cool place for twenty-four hours, or longer, should it not then appear perfectly curdled. Pour it gently into a fine hair-sieve, and let the clear juice drain through without pressure; pass it through a jelly-bag, or a closely-woven cloth, weigh it, and add as much *good* sugar broken small as there is of the juice, and when this is dissolved turn the syrup into a preserving-pan or stewpan, and boil it gently for four or five minutes being careful to clear off all the scum. In twelve hours afterwards the syrup may be put into small dry bottles, and corked and stored in a cool, but dry place. It is a most agreeable preparation, retaining perfectly the flavour of the fresh fruit; and mixed with water, it affords, like strawberry or raspberry vinegar, a delicious summer beverage, and one which is peculiarly adapted to invalids. It makes also a fine isinglass jelly, and an incomparable sweet-pudding sauce. A portion of raspberry or cherry-juice may be mixed with that of the currants at pleasure.

## CHERRY-BRANDY
### (*Tappington Everard Receipt*)

Fill to about two-thirds of their depth, some wide-necked bottles with the small cherries called in the markets brandy-blacks; pour in sufficient sifted sugar to fill up more than half of the remaining space, and then as much good French brandy as will cover the fruit, and reach to the necks of the bottles. Cork them securely, and let them stand for two months before they are opened: the liqueur poured from the cherries will be excellent, and the fruit itself very good.

## OXFORD RECEIPT FOR BISHOP

'Make several incisions in the rind of a lemon, stick cloves in these, and roast the lemon by a slow fire. Put small but equal quantities of cinnamon, cloves, mace, and allspice, with a race of ginger, into a saucepan with half a pint of water: let it boil until it is reduced one-half. Boil one bottle of port wine, burn a portion of the spirit out of it by applying a lighted paper to the saucepan; put the roasted lemon and spice into the wine; stir it up well, and let it stand near the fire ten minutes. Rub a few knobs of sugar on the rind of a lemon, put the sugar into a bowl or jug, with the juice of half a lemon (not roasted), pour the wine into it, grate in some nutmeg, sweeten it to the taste, and serve it up with the lemon and spice floating in it.'

*Obs.* Bishop is frequently made with a Seville orange stuck with cloves and slowly roasted, and its flavour to many tastes is infinitely finer than that of the lemon.

## CAMBRIDGE MILK PUNCH

Throw into two quarts of new milk the very thinly-pared rind of a fine lemon, and half a pound of good sugar in lumps; bring it slowly to boil, take out the lemon-rind, draw it from the fire, and stir quickly in a couple of well-whisked eggs which have been mixed with less than half a pint of cold milk, and strained through a sieve; the milk must not of course be allowed to boil after these are mixed with it. Add gradually a pint of rum, and half a pint of brandy; mill the punch to a froth, and serve it immediately with quite warm glasses. At the University the lemon-rind is usually omitted, but it is a great improvement to the flavour of the beverage. The sugar and spirit can be otherwise apportioned to the taste; and we would recommend the yolks of three eggs, or of four, in preference to the two whole ones.

New milk, 2 quarts; rind, 1 large lemon; sugar, ½ lb; fresh eggs, 2; cold milk, ⅓ pint: rum, 1 pint; brandy, ½ pint.

## TO MULL WINE
### (*An excellent French Receipt*)

Boil in a wineglassful and a half of water, a quarter of an ounce of spice (cinnamon, ginger slightly bruised, and cloves), with three ounces of fine sugar, until they form a thick syrup, which must not on any account be allowed to burn. Pour in a pint of port wine, and stir it gently until it is on the *point* of boiling only: it should then be served immediately. The addition of a strip or two of orange-rind cut extremely thin, gives to this beverage the flavour of Bishop. In France light claret takes the place of port wine in making it, and the better kinds of *vin ordinaire* are very palatable thus prepared.

Water, 1½ wineglassful; spice, ¼ oz, of which fine cloves, 24, and of remainder, rather more ginger than cinnamon; sugar, 3 oz: 15 to 20 minutes. Port wine or claret, 1 pint; orange-rind, if used, to be boiled with the spice.

*Obs.* Sherry, or very fine raisin or ginger wine, prepared as above, and stirred hot to the yolks of four fresh eggs, will make good egg-wine.

## AN ADMIRABLE COOL CUP

Weigh six ounces of sugar in lumps, and extract the essence from the rind of a large fresh lemon by rubbing them upon it; then put them into a deep jug, and add the strained juice of one lemon and a half. When the sugar is dissolved, pour in a bottle of good cider, and three large wineglassesful of sherry: add nearly half a small nutmeg lightly grated, and serve the cup with or without some sprigs of fresh balm or borage in it. Brandy is sometimes added to it, but is, we think, no improvement. If closely covered down, and placed on ice for a short time, it will be more agreeable as a summer beverage.

## EXCELLENT PORTABLE LEMONADE

Rasp, with a quarter-pound of sugar, the rind of a very fine juicy lemon, reduce it to powder, and pour on it the strained juice of the fruit. Press the mixture into a jar, and when wanted for use dissolve a tablespoonful of it in a glass of water. It will keep a considerable time. If too sweet for the taste of the drinker, a very small portion of citric acid may be added when it is taken.

## RAISIN WINE, WHICH, IF LONG KEPT, REALLY RESEMBLES FOREIGN

First boil the water which is to be used for the wine, and let it again become perfectly cold; then put into a sound sweet cask eight pounds of fine Malaga raisins for each gallon that is to be used, taking out only the quite large stalks; the fruit and water may be put in alternately until the cask is full, the raisins being well pressed down in it; lay the bung lightly over, stir the wine every day or two, and keep it full by the addition of water that has, like the first, been boiled, but which must always be quite cold when it is used. So soon as the fermentation has entirely ceased, which may be in from six to seven weeks, press in the bung, and leave the wine untouched for twelve months; draw it off then into a clean cask, and fine it, if necessary, with isinglass, tied in a muslin and suspended in it. We have not ourselves had this receipt tried; but we have tasted wine made by it which had been five years kept, and which so much resembled a rich foreign wine that we could with difficulty believe it was English-made.

To each gallon of water (boiled and left till cold) 8 lb of fine Malaga raisins; to stand 12 months; then to be drawn off and fined.

*Obs.* The refuse raisins make admirable vinegar if

fresh water be poured to them, and the cask placed in the sun. March is the best time for making the wine.

## THE COUNSELLOR'S CUP

Rub a quarter of a pound of sugar upon the rinds of two fine China oranges, put it into an enamelled stewpan, and pour on it a pint of water; let these boil gently for two or three minutes, then pour on half a pint of China orange-juice mixed with that of one lemon, and previously strained through muslin; the moment this begins to boil, pour it into a hot jug, and stir to it half a pint of the best Cognac brandy. Serve it immediately. When preferred cold, prepare the syrup with the juice of the fruit, cover it down in the jug, set it into ice, or into a very cool place, and add the spirit only just before the cup is wanted for table. Should the fruit be very acid, increase the proportion of sugar. A few slight strips of the rind of a Seville orange cut very thin, would to many tastes be an agreeable addition to the beverage; which should be made always with fresh sound fruit.

Sugar, 4 oz (6 if needed); rasped rinds of China oranges, 2; water, 1 pint: 3 minutes. Strained juice of China oranges mixed with that of 1 large lemon, ½ pint; best Cognac brandy, ½ pint.

*Obs.* For a large cup these proportions must be doubled. Sherry or Madeira substituted for the brandy, will make a pleasant cool cup of this kind; and equal parts of well made lemonade, and of any good light white wine, thoroughly cooled down, will give another agreeable beverage for warm weather; but a much smaller proportion of wine would better adapt it to many tastes.

# GREAT  FOOD

THROUGHOUT the history of civilization, food has been livelihood, status symbol, entertainment – and passion. The twenty fine food writers here, reflecting on different cuisines from across the centuries and around the globe, have influenced each other and continue to influence us today, opening the door to the wonders of every kitchen.